# INVESTING THE INVESTMENT CLUB WAY

By joining or forming investment clubs, anyone from any background can become a shrewd stock market investor. From picking the right companies to managing your trading costs, this book gives you all the information—including a complete glossary and resource list—you need to start investing.

**LEARN**

- Why more than 60 percent of investment clubs regularly beat the performance of the Standard & Poor's 500 index
- How your club should choose a broker and get your money's worth from commissions
- How clubs are organized and run for maximum return on the dollar
- How clubs decide to buy stocks—and when to sell them
- How to analyze companies to see the growth and profit potential—no matter what the stock market is doing
- How to diversify your club's portfolio and reinvest dividends
- The Five Habits of Highly Effective Investment Clubs—for long-term stability and success.

"A useful guide for taking charge of your financial life. John Wasik has written a book full of practical information for anyone interested in starting or joining an investment club."

— Joseph Anthony, financial writer, author of
*Working for Yourself: Full Time, Part Time, Anytime*

An Alternate Selection of The Literary Guild®
and a Featured Alternate Selection of Doubleday Book Club®

*please turn this page for more rave reviews*

"What a great book! It is time that the individual be shown how to truly safeguard their future and invest with intelligence. This book does exactly that. If you want to secure your retirement, read this book."

—Suze Orman, CFP, author of
*You've Earned It, Don't Lose It!*

"If you invest on a shoestring, then this is the book for you. No more feeling left behind by all those wealthy Wall Street aristocrats. John Wasik uncovers some of the hottest secrets to investing and teaches you how to become your own tycoon."

—Christy Heady, syndicated and financial journalist,
author of *The Complete Guide to
Making Money on Wall Street*

# THE INVE$TMENT CLUB BOOK

by John F. Wasik

**WARNER BOOKS**

A Time Warner Company

Warner Books, Inc., 1271 Avenue of the Americas,
New York, NY 10020

W A Time Warner Company

First printing: November 1995

10  9  8  7  6  5  4  3  2  1

Library of Congress Cataloging-in-Publication Data

Wasik, John F.
    The investment club book / John F. Wasik.
        p.   cm.
    Includes index.
    ISBN 0-446-67147-9
    1. Investment clubs—United States.   2. Investments—United
States.   I. Title.
HG4530.W37   1995
332.6'78—dc20                                        95-15931
                                                          CIP

Interior design by Charles Sutherland
Cover design by Bernadette Anthony

**TO KATHLEEN,
WHOSE PATIENCE AND LOVE
COMPOUND OVER TIME.**

Thanks to all of the wonderful people of the NAIC, especially Tom O'Hara, Ken Janke, Martha Moore, and Ralph Seger. And, of course, to investment clubbers everywhere.

All materials obtained from the National Association of Investors Corporation are used with permission.

Charts used with permission from Ibbotson Associates, Chicago, from *Stocks, Bonds, Bills and Inflation 1994 Yearbook* (annual updates by Roger Ibbotson and Rex A. Sinquefield). All rights reserved.

# CONTENTS

# FOREWORD

In the thirty-five years that I have been involved in investing, perhaps a thousand books on the subject have found their way to my desk, ranging from cattle futures to the potential downfall of the American economy. Most have centered on how to invest in myriad financial instruments with chapter headings that can almost be predicted without going beyond the cover. They have contained all kinds of different theories and formulas to make the investor more successful. What I have discovered, however, is that successful investing comes from common sense. Investing is not mysterious. John Wasik has been able to capture that common sense from people who invest, using time-tested principles that may appear simple on the surface but when followed produce superior results. Instead of only a "how to" book, he offers a "how they did it" book, where the reader has an opportunity to learn firsthand how different people made their investment decisions. He has added the human factor.

It has long been my contention that an individual can take every investment course that is offered through adult education and various brokerage firms and still not know how to invest. That experience comes only when the individual puts money at risk, whether it's a large sum or $30 each month. In surveys taken by NAIC over the years, we have consistently found that in a newly formed investment club of fifteen members, only one or two have ever invested before the club was organized. After five years, the figures are completely reversed. All of the members, except for one or two, are not only continuing in their club, but are investing on their own, building individual portfolios and investing three times as much as in their club. Investment clubs serve as an introduction to the stock market. By investing on their own, they are able to build sizable nest eggs for retirement or other needs. But the investment club account itself can turn into a bonanza if it's a lifetime project.

In the Mutual Investment Club of Detroit, which was founded in 1940, one of the original members began by investing $10 each month and then increased that amount to $20. Upon retirement, he withdrew $70,000 to pay off his mortgage and become debt free. Even though he is retired, he continues to invest and participate in the club activities. Through the years his out-of-pocket investment has been less than $10,000, yet his total worth in the investment club is now $570,000. His experience has served as an example for the younger members who have joined the investment club in recent years.

At times the professional investment community, with some notable exceptions, has passed off investment club members as amateurs who get lucky now and then. Yet those professionals have been unable to argue with the clubs' success. On these pages you will be able to meet real people who make real decisions. That's important, because there's more to investing than simply trying to use some formula.

John has visited with clubs, attending their meetings as well as the investor fairs and other seminars that are held for the benefit of club members and individual investors. He has invested himself and is even part of a family investment club. The result is that John has been able to impart real-life investing experiences in this book. From all of this, he has learned why some are successful while others fail, and that information is passed along to the reader in a manner that makes it not only interesting, but informative. If you belong to an investment club, you will easily be able to relate to various incidents. If you don't belong, it probably won't be very long before you organize one of your own. I hope so. It's a wonderful experience.

—Kenneth S. Janke
President and CEO
NAIC (National Association of
Investors Corporation)

# PREFACE

This book is about hundreds of thousands of people who weren't born with money, didn't invent anything, didn't build a successful business, didn't win the lottery. They started out with as little as $10 a month and built it into sizable sums using some simple yet elegant rules. Profitable stock investing as perfected by thousands of investment clubs throughout the world is hardly a fluke. This "movement" has created at least one hundred millionaires and countless thousands who are able to retire in comfort, buy second homes, and send their children to college. I've talked to clubs from coast to coast, attended investment fairs and seminars, and visited the headquarters of organized investment clubs in an effort to distill some of their methods. There is no one secret to winning big, but a handful of strategies is enough to guide you along the path to a kind of successful investing rarely seen on Wall Street.

The only sure thing about the knowledge in this book is that if you don't apply the basic tools of investing, make some mistakes, learn from them, and consistently monitor what you're doing over *decades*, you'll get frustrated and go back to buying lottery tickets every week. If you do follow a pattern of quality, long-term investing, you'll be well on your way to a financially secure future. Yet when it comes to one of the most durable ways of making money over the long term, most people ignore this tantalizing investment strategy.

If you're expecting these strategies to work overnight, this book is not for you. You may wait years for this kind of investing to pay off. But it's worth the wait.

I first became interested in investment clubs because some interesting material crossed my desk at *Consumers Digest* some three years ago. It had to do with how groups of ordinary people were picking their own stocks, investing small sums of money — and profiting consistently over the years. Many were outperforming the top investors on Wall Street. To a seasoned financial journalist, this seemed an absurd idea at first. How could people outside the investment community make money by picking common stocks? I thought. Wouldn't they be too impatient to stick by their choices through thick and thin? Worse yet, wouldn't they get toasted because they weren't trading on Wall Street with their ears to the track?

So I did a short piece on investing alternatives for *Consumers Digest*. I interviewed Tom O'Hara, the genial chairman of the National Association of Investors Corporation (NAIC), and gave a short mention of the group in the piece. Although I'm fairly diligent about including addresses and phone numbers when I mention a resource, I neglected to do so in this article. After the piece ran, I found out firsthand about the appeal of investment clubs. My phone rang off the hook for *three weeks*. Everybody wanted to know where they could find this group. I must have logged several hundred responses. In eighteen years as a journalist, it was the greatest response I'd ever received to anything I wrote—or, rather, didn't write. That episode convinced me that there was something more to these investment clubs. So what did I do? First I pitched a story on clubs to my editors, with no success. Then I joined the NAIC as an individual member. I learned a lot and lost a lot, but, following investment club principles, I was able to profit from my knowledge (for my results, see the epilogue). I also impressed my wife, Kathleen, who started a club for us and our immediate family.

About one year after doing the magazine piece, inspired by the high success rate of clubs, I began writing this book. Along the way, I discovered much of what makes conscientious amateur investors the sharpest in the world. They do their homework. They're not afraid to take a risk as long as it's measured over time. And they are supporting the very structure of capitalism in the process. By taking risks, they're helping to preserve and create jobs. If they stay the course, they are rewarded immensely for their small portfolios. Except for an occasional amen to Peter Lynch, there's no religion involved in the process. They just want what everyone who wasn't born with money wants: security and a comfortable life.

This book is for investors at *any* level who feel they can learn and earn in a club setting—or by themselves. Whether you plan to start or join a club, or you are already in one, you can benefit from this volume.

Use the index and table of contents to spot areas of interest. Since this book wasn't meant to be read exclusively from beginning to end (unless you're a total novice), feel free to browse.

If you feel that your biggest problem is getting off the ground, start with the epilogue, where you'll find lots of basic savings tips.

Then begin at the beginning and work your way through. If you feel you're an intermediate to advanced investor, try the chapters on stock picking, cycles, and brokers. You'll find some useful information there. Most of all, enjoy. And profit from the experience.

# PART I

# The Power of
# Investment Clubs

It doesn't take an investment genius to beat professional investors and mutual fund managers. Two-thirds of them don't beat the average market performance anyway. The secret to long-term profits is that there is no one secret. Success comes with diligence.

Nearly half of all investment clubs regularly outperform professionals and beat the average return for the stock market. And you can do the same. Others have from all walks of life. And they've done it consistently and safely, using conservative strategies. For example, the Beardstown Ladies' Club has attained such fame for its streak of winning investment club contests that it's been on national television, produced a video, and written a book. This small group of middle-aged and older women, based near Peoria, Illinois, has had extraordinary success over more than ten years of investing. Their average annual return has been 23.4 percent. Their prime secret: "We do our homework."

Ironically, club members have been a victim of the Beardstown Ladies' success. The NAIC has suspended its annual performance contest because too many clubs got frustrated over their inability to match the Ladies' results.

Fortunately, those with the least amount of knowledge—and the greatest desire to learn—do the best in investment clubs. No one race, gender, profession, or creed has a lock on what it takes to make money through stock investing. In fact, investors who are not located near major financial centers seem to do the best. Why is club investing a good idea? There seems to be strength in numbers.

All told, there are more than 14,000 clubs in the United States that are affiliated with the NAIC, plus uncounted thousands that operate independently. And some fifty-one million individual investors work outside of U.S. clubs.

Even more remarkable is the fact that often more than half of the investment clubs surveyed beat the stock market (as measured by the Standard & Poor's 500 index). The majority of them started out with very small investments of as little as ten dollars a month per person.

In clubs and by themselves, individual investors are flaunting the conventional wisdom that most people lose money in the stock market. Simply put, they are "cookie jar" investors. They invest small amounts relatively conservatively, but they research their investments carefully. Over time, they are rewarded by the superior returns from stocks. They are able to retire comfortably and finance college educations or dream vacation homes.

You don't even need to have a group of people to benefit from the investment clubs. In fact, you can do it yourself or with your spouse or significant other. All it requires is a commitment to save on a regular basis and to learn the successful techniques.

Although there are investment clubs in every state and across the world, some 20 percent of U.S.-based clubs are located in the "heartland" states of Michigan, Ohio, Indiana, and Illinois. All kinds of people are active members, from teachers to retired grandmothers, engineers to janitors: these organizations don't require business school résumés, special handshakes, secret oaths, or funny hats. The one thing their members have in common is a simple devotion to learning about investing.

Unlike the profiles of most stock investors, the profiles of investment clubs are as diverse as the world itself. Clubs include janitors, engineers, truck drivers, housewives, musicians, beauticians, professors, and maintenance workers. There's scarcely an ethnic, professional, religious, or socioeconomic group that's not represented. In speaking to more than twenty investment fairs

---

**Investfact: NAIC Profile**

- Total personal portfolio of all
  NAIC members. . . . . . . . . . . . . . . . $20.3 billion
- Average NAIC club portfolio. . . . . . . . . . $89,010
- Average personal portfolio
  (outside of club) . . . . . . . . . . . . . . . . . . $110,000
- Number of clubs over twenty
  years old . . . . . . . . . . . . . . . . . . . . . . . 1,000 plus
- Percentage of men and
  women in clubs. . . . . . . . . . . . . . . . 49.6%/50.4%

---

throughout the country every year, Ken Janke has come across clubs that comprise priests, members of Lawrence Welk's band (the "Champagne Investors"), infield maintenance workers for the Philadelphia Phillies, and public school custodians. "Success in a club is not related to their background," Janke notes.

The investment club concept has universal appeal. Despite the fact that the NAIC doesn't advertise, they receive some 76,000 inquiries a year. Some 4,000 people a month join up for their low-cost stock purchase program alone.

There are other personal investment organizations in the United States. The Chicago-based American Association of Individual Investors (see the resources section at back of book), for example, provides a fine program of educational materials and seminars. They too have more than 150,000 members.

# CHAPTER 1

# Investing for Peace of Mind

Larry Carlson is just one example of what club investing can accomplish. He long believed that his best chance for a comfortable retirement involved investing in the stock market. Since 1970 the former Vermont paper industry engineer has been following the National Association of Investors Corporation (NAIC) investing format as an individual member. Picking good stocks at an early age helped him achieve an annual average return of 18 percent. He's confident that he's beaten most professionals at their own game. He did this through discipline and starting out small—$100 every three months, starting in 1966. Having amassed a seven-figure portfolio, he retired *early*.

Saving from 5 percent to 20 percent of his pay, he started his investment plan in his twenties, picking stocks with ample growth potential and reinvesting the dividends. Although some of his picks soared due to pure luck, the rest grew prodigiously simply because they were good companies—and he never sold them.

One of his hottest stocks—U.S. Tobacco—is what he terms a "ten bagger." It's appreciated some twelve times beyond what he

**5**

originally invested in it. Another pick (made by his wife) was a company called Daxor, which specialized in frozen blood supplies. Fueled by the AIDS (tainted) blood scare, the stock zoomed 700 percent within two weeks of purchase.

Although he's held some dogs (A. H. Robins and Bolar, to name two), he's built his portfolio through long holding periods and refusing to get spooked when the market turned south. He says he's held his best stocks—like Pepsico, Abbott, Kellogg, Johnson & Johnson, and Quaker Oats—some fifteen to twenty years. As he puts it: "As long as they're meeting my objectives and making progress, I hold 'em."

For more than eleven years he's enhanced his stock-picking skills by using a computer. The computer helps him screen out good picks from the more than 7,600 stocks in a database provided by the American Association of Individual Investors (AAII), which provides research and educational materials to amateur investors (see resources section in back of book). He also uses the group's materials to find small-company stocks, which constitute 20 percent of his portfolio and tend to lower overall risk.

"I've found peace of mind [through stock investing]," Carlson says. "I'm not counting on Social Security as we know it. I stressed my own investing even more. I wanted to retire before I was fifty."

His straightforward Yankee advice is typical of that offered by both the NAIC and the American Association of Individual Investors. Although Wall Street no doubt cringes at the mention of it, hundreds of thousands of individual investors are beating the market—and doing it consistently by picking their own stocks. The following strategies have proven profitable for Carlson and for thousands of diligent investors across the country:

- Invest in companies you know rather than highfliers. Stay away from penny stocks and brokers' picks (see page 49).
- Even if you buy one share of a company, reinvest the dividends; they just keep building up in dividend reinvestment plans (see page 163).
- Initially find a stock that'll grow for five to ten years.
- Don't follow business cycles (when buying). Dollar-cost average and keep investing on a regular basis in the bad part of business cycles (see page 185).
- Go with companies that have good earnings in both up and down years.

## DON'T LET THE STOCK MARKET SCARE YOU

Even with odds of more than ten *million* to one, millions of sure losers line up every week for lottery tickets. But when you mention the stock market, most people turn up their noses and tell you it's too risky. Even if they're not thinking of winning the jackpot, they'd rather bet on a *sure* thing: federally insured savings accounts. Again, they're betting on sure losers, since these accounts rarely beat inflation, meaning they consistently lose money over time when you subtract taxes and inflation.

But consider this: If you were to invest in common stocks for just five years, you stand an 89 percent chance of making money, according to Ibbotson Associates. Over twenty years your chances grow to 100 percent. That's a sure thing (based on historical data). And that's just with a breadbasket of five hundred stocks bought and not touched. Imagine if you carefully picked a portfolio and a handful of your stocks did really well. It just takes time and patience.

By investing on a regular basis over decades, you can ride through the downturns and buy stocks at lower prices when others are selling. It's that simple.

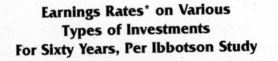

## Earnings Rates* on Various Types of Investments For Sixty Years, Per Ibbotson Study

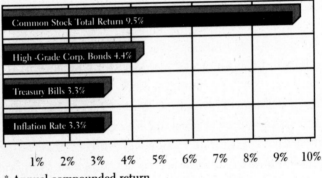

|  |  |  |  |  |  |  |  |  |  |
| --- | --- | --- | --- | --- | --- | --- | --- | --- | --- |
| 1% | 2% | 3% | 4% | 5% | 6% | 7% | 8% | 9% | 10% |

Common Stock Total Return 9.5%

High-Grade Corp. Bonds 4.4%

Treasury Bills 3.3%

Inflation Rate 3.3%

\* Annual compounded return

## INVESTMENT CLUBS ARE A LEARNING EXPERIENCE

John Paterson is another example of investment club success. Although he is eighty-one years old and one of the leading investment clubbers in the Seattle area today, he can remember a time when he bought AT&T because it was the only stock he knew and it paid a 9 percent dividend. The psychology of money is a peculiar one that invokes the most intense love-hate relationships. Investing is an activity that most of us fear for all the right reasons. We look for the safest, surest vehicle there is, believing the sales pitches and ignoring the real returns. But John somehow overcame the conventional wisdom.

"I didn't even know why, I just went down to the bank and bought it [AT&T]. I didn't even follow up."

But when Tom O'Hara, one of the founding NAIC members, came through town in 1961, Paterson saw stock investing in a different light. So he started the "Blue Chip" club, adhering religiously to NAIC techniques. The former navy engineer was working at a Seattle shipyard at the time and contacted men he knew from the Boy Scouts. His club of thirteen families has not only padded several nest eggs—including his own—it prospered with "local" stocks such as Microsoft (now the club's largest holding). His son, Tim, also a member, was one of the original authors of Microsoft's breakthrough MS-DOS program.

Before almost anyone knew what a personal computer was, John had already begun developing investment software, including an accounting and stock selection package in 1978. When his investment club was organized, he invited only friends and people he knew from work. All fourteen original members were men.

"It was a great shock for us to discover, in the down market of 1962, that stocks went down as well as up. However, we stayed together and found the value of dollar [cost] averaging as the market rose the following year."

The market did more than rise in successive years. Paterson recalls that in 1972 the club made its first payout to members— about $4,000 each. Then they reorganized, set the minimum monthly investment at $20 (up from $10), and invited women to join. Today, although only three of the original members are still in the club, their sixteen members representing twelve families share in a $240,000 portfolio.

John repeats the refrain of investors from Seattle to Ft. Lauderdale: "The club is primarily a learning experience. Most members have their own portfolios that represent many times the investment of clubs. Whether or not a club makes money is of secondary importance. The learning experience is what counts." Here's a sampling of some of their best picks, good examples of buying low and holding on:

## The Blue Chip Club

| Stock | Buy | Current Price* | Avg. Return |
|---|---|---|---|
| Abbott Labs | $5.74 | $31.25 | 18% |
| Cardinal Health Inc. | $28.73 | $50.87 | 53% |
| Microsoft | $8.26 | $52.87 | 49% |
| Vishay Inter. | $15.79 | $38.50 | 41% |
| Wendy's | $13.94 | $17.25 | 22% |

*"Current" price is price as of this writing. For updated price, check the current quotes in the financial section of your newspaper. Prices don't indicate stock splits.

## BEATING THE MONEY MIND GAME

This book shows how investment clubs make stock market investing accessible to anyone. So why is it that when it comes to saving and investing for the future, something almost ingrained in human nature seems to suggest we can't be successful at it? One common refrain is "I'm just no good when it comes to money."

Maybe you can blame the Puritans. Talking about money in groups was never seen as socially acceptable in the eyes of the priggish Pilgrims. Phrases like "Money is the root of all evil" and other biblical bromides have permeated the public consciousness, to our detriment. It's been one of those perverse love-hate relationships. We'd all love to have more money, but we hate to discuss it honestly. And the specter of the Great Depression hasn't helped most Americans overcome their fear of investing. Investment clubs, however, have confronted those fears rationally and set people on the path to financial security.

Human genome (gene-mapping) studies will doubtless show that there is no such thing as a "bad money" gene. People want to believe that they're bad with money so that they don't have to deal with it or take responsibility for managing it. Many books have been written on this subject alone, so I won't get into it here. The fact is that anyone willing seriously to wade into investing can master a few basic techniques.

Don Danko, a longtime NAIC member and editor of the group's *Better Investing* magazine, thinks that despite society's failings on financial education, the need for social contact and self-improvement can make anyone a profitable investor. Every year his magazine reviews some of the top clubs in the country for their "All-Star" ranking. The clubs are chosen not so much for their performance (although they are consistently excellent), but for the quality of the education programs they produce. Don notes that the leading quality all successful clubs have is "the desire to be together." As he notes, "Everything else is a close second."

Coming from a professional money management background, Don joined a club thinking that he would have more answers than questions. But he readily admits that he learned patience and perseverance being in a club. Today he proudly claims that in addition to being financially comfortable, "our child will go to college based on our McDonald's stock holding alone."

He laughs at the times people ask him for stock picks at parties and then show their disdain when he suggests unglamorous long-term investments. In the same breath, he's appalled at the growth of gambling. Across the Detroit River (near where he works) in Windsor, Canada, they're planning to open twenty-four-hour gambling facilities. "It just consumes," he says with a sigh.

Unfortunately, gambling is a prime example of the "quick fix" approach too many people take to their finances. If that sounds like you, you have to "unlearn" a number of myths and behaviors before the concept of wealth can become a realistic notion. Once this happens, anyone can become wealthy within a lifetime. But first let's dispatch some nasty fiction of Western consumerism:

- **Fable:** Someone or something will suddenly appear in your life to relieve all of your financial fears—inheritances, lotteries, contests, game shows, and large windfalls in improbable schemes.
- **Reality Bite:** While fairy tales can come true, they happen so rarely that it's wise not to wait for the phone to ring. You can, however, take control of your financial destiny. Nothing's written in stone in this age of information. You can, however, invest long term and profit—no matter who you are or where you come from. *All kinds of people invest successfully on their own and in clubs.*

- **Fable:** Social Security, pension plans, your home's value, life insurance, and family bequests will take care of you in retirement.
- **Reality Bite:** Unless your family's rich to begin with and the

party bequeathing the money remembers you kindly in his/her will, all of these scenarios are unreliable. Merrill Lynch reports that today's average fifty-year-old has set aside a measly $2,300 for retirement. You can, however, start your own retirement plan and do quite well with it over time. *You need no previous experience.*

- Fable: Brokers, financial planners, mutual funds, insurers, and "Uncle Ernie" will all take care of my finances and make me rich.
- Reality Bite: All people, including Uncle Ernie, are capitalists, not philanthropists. They typically make more money than you do off of the junk they sell you. But you can fill nearly all of your financial needs yourself, and you can do so while meeting educational and social needs as well — in an investment club experience, which teaches you how to manage better consistently, year after year. Remember, most club investment members have six-figure personal portfolios. *You can build a substantial portfolio by yourself.*

---

Investfact: Clubs consisting of all women outperform all men's clubs in terms of portfolio returns, but coed clubs outperform the single-sex groups, according to the NAIC.

---

# CHAPTER 2

# Two Good Reasons to Invest in Stocks

## THE BEST REASON: YOUR PENSION

Don't procrastinate investing on your own because you think your employer will take care of you. Thousands upon thousands of people have lost their private pensions, even though they believed they had the most ironclad union contracts and government insurance guaranteeing them.

On a chilly morning in March of 1980, some 3,400 workers at the Wisconsin Steel Works on the South Side of Chicago discovered that their plant had closed unexpectedly. But they were confident that the padlocks would come off the front gate any day and they would be back at work with full benefits. But when the holding companies that owned the plant filed for Chapter 11 bankruptcy, the Chase Manhattan Bank seized all the money in the payroll account as collateral for a loan, and the workers' pensions fell through the cracks of a hundred documents.

The Wisconsin Steel workers' union was represented by a powerful Chicago lawyer and alderman. Their pension plan had even been set up by one of the bastions of industry in Chicago (at the time), the International Harvester Corporation. But because of a punishing recession that was forcing the restructuring of all of American industry, Harvester, too, was devastated. Wisconsin Steel never reopened and fell into the hands of the federal government. After a decade of legal wrangling with Harvester (which became Navistar), attorney Thomas Geoghegan managed to win back most of the workers' pension benefits. It also helped that former millworker Frank Lumpkin kept the workers pressing their legal claims. But by that time a large percentage of the workers had either become chronically unemployed or underemployed or had died poor.

What happened at Wisconsin Steel is still happening today, and on a broader scale. Companies are phasing out their expensive defined-benefit (DB) plans in place of either no-pension or defined-contribution (DC) plans. Now the dinosaur of corporate benefits, DB plans promised to pay retirees a set amount for the rest of their lives, based upon complex formulas that figured in years of service, wages, and vesting requirements.

As a result of the contraction of Western industry, employees have been forced to take on more of the risk in providing for their own retirement. Defined-contribution plans like 401(k)s make employees responsible for choosing the right mutual funds for long-term investment. That translates into nearly full responsibility for a personal portfolio that's not guaranteed by any agency at any time.

The Pension Benefit Guaranty Corporation (PBGC) is a government agency mandated to insure large DB plans like the one at Wisconsin Steel. Like the Federal Deposit Insurance Corporation, it collects premiums from companies and pools them into an insurance fund in case large companies collapse and can't pay off their pension obligations. But like many government insurance programs, it too is underfunded. A "big hit" by a large company (such as LTV or Pan Am) forces them into court—often for years—to sue the bankrupt company to pay off pensions.

Most large companies don't fully fund their pension plans, since full funding would cover all of their employees collecting pension benefits tomorrow, which is highly unlikely. But if a company isn't putting enough money into a pension plan and runs into another recession, market downshift, or inflationary cycle, it could run short when it comes to massive retirements.

## Largest Underfunded Pension Plans

| Company | Assets | UGB | GFR |
|---|---|---|---|
| LTV | $1,273 | $1,933 | 40% |
| Uniroyal Goodrich | 517 | 450 | 53% |
| Rockwell Int'l | 462 | 344 | 57% |
| TransWorld Air | 592 | 426 | 58% |
| Bridgestone-Firestone | 303 | 217 | 58% |
| Bethlehem Steel | 3,426 | 2,138 | 62% |
| General Motors | 39,572 | 17,195 | 70% |
| Westinghouse | 3,918 | 1,012 | 79% |
| Goodyear Tire | 1,276 | 265 | 83% |
| Chrysler | 8,332 | 876 | 90% |

All assets in millions. UGB = unfunded guaranteed benefit, which is the shortfall in pension funds for the benefits guaranteed by the Pension Benefit Guaranty Corporation (PBGC). GFR = guaranteed funding ratio, or the percentage of guaranteed benefits the company has funded. All figures through 1992, the most recently available year. For current figures, call the PBGC at (202) 778-8840 to request the *Top 50 Companies with the Largest Unfunded Pension Liabilities*. Source: PBGC, Standard & Poor's Compustat services.

In researching an article on pension plans, I used the Freedom of Information Act to unearth PBGC records of the fifty largest underfunded pension plans. The list I came up with read like a *Who's Who* of big manufacturers and service concerns. Among them were GM, Goodyear, Kellogg's, United Air Lines, and Westinghouse. To date the list has changed little, although most companies have ponied up more money for their pension plans as their financial health has improved.

The PBGC notes that "inclusion on the list does not reflect on a company's financial health, nor does it necessarily mean that a participant's benefits are in immediate jeopardy. However, the risk is greater when underfunding occurs in plans of troubled companies. Although a majority of retirees are fully covered if their plan terminates, there are limits to PBGC's guarantees."

If another recession wreaks havoc on these heavy industries—or if these companies fail to compete in the world market—the government and employees get the short end of the stick on pensions they thought were guaranteed for life. A numbers game is also playing against the maintenance of huge pension plans. The number of older and retired workers is outnumbering those in the workforce contributing to pension funds.

*The New York Times* summarized the situation by using Ford as an example. In 1950 Ford had "sixty-two active workers for each retiree. Now that ratio is 1.2 to 1. Industrywide, there are almost as many retired autoworkers as active ones. . . ."

What seemed to be a trickle nearly a decade ago is now a flood of pension cutbacks. More than forty-two thousand employers terminated defined-benefit plans between 1989 and 1991 alone, according to a survey of the American Academy of Actuaries. That's an increase of 300 percent over the first three years of the

1980s—a period that takes in the tail end of a recession. In one-third of the cases, workers received less generous coverage.

In summary, you can't depend on your company pension plan to be your sole source of retirement income. Although chances are good it'll be there for you, nothing's truly guaranteed.

---

Investfact: Some fourteen million workers are being forced to accept reduced benefits, according to the Employers Council on Flexible Compensation. All told, some thirty-five thousand firms have terminated their DB plans since 1990.

---

## THE SECOND MOST IMPORTANT REASON: SOCIAL SECURITY AND ITS SHORTFALL

There are two realities to Social Security as we now know it. If you're currently receiving benefits, it's the best deal in the world. Even taking into account inflation, Americans are now getting twenty times more in Social Security retirement benefits than the first recipients were paid more than fifty years ago.

But if you're still in the workforce, you're paying dearly for this inflation-adjusted bonanza—and you might not be able to reap this windfall yourself. Check your pay stub: chances are you're now paying more in Social Security and Medicare taxes (FICA) than in federal income tax. If you're waiting for Social Security to provide for your retirement in a few decades, however, you're in trouble.

Dorcas Hardy, the commissioner of the Social Security Administration under President Reagan, is sounding the alarm about the future of Social Security. Her view is that unless the program is restructured, the system will run out of money between 2020 and 2030. That's because by the year 2005 there'll only be one worker for every retiree, versus three workers per retiree now. More money will be coming out of the system than will be put back in.

The most pressing retirement problem, Ms. Hardy notes, doesn't even involve Social Security. We are simply living longer. Statistics show that, on average, you could live another twenty to thirty years past retirement. According to IRS mortality tables, the average retiree today can expect to live to age seventy-five and has a 50 percent chance of reaching ninety. The fastest-growing age group is centenarians. That means some of us will have to save enough to support ourselves for nearly another working life. No wonder a Gallup poll found that some 40 percent of Americans expect to outlive their nest eggs.

Ms. Hardy is one of the first to dismiss the many myths of Social Security.

First, it's not a pension system. Most people will get back all the money they put into it within three years of retiring. "From then on, the retiree is receiving what amounts to a government dole!"

More important, Social Security is not a trust fund that's protecting and investing your money until you need it. "The fact remains, the taxes you pay today are not invested for your future retirement; they are used primarily to pay benefits to current retirees." So there's no account with your name on it. You can't withdraw upon demand every dollar you've put into it when you retire. The government's using your money to pay its bills and sticks IOUs in the form of Treasury bills back into the system.

For future retirees, Social Security is the worst imaginable savings account. The funds withdrawn from your paycheck for the system (roughly 7.5 percent of yearly income, 15 percent if you're self-employed) are invested in T-bills, but that doesn't mean you receive compounded interest. Benefits are fixed every year based on inflation. You can't do any better than that formula. Since you *don't* have any control over how this money is invested, you can't increase the monthly amount even if the cost of living is one hundred times higher than today.

Just think what you could do if you could invest that money at 12 percent a year for thirty years. A two-income household paying $11,000 a year in Social Security taxes would double their money in six years. After thirty years that adds up to $369,600 on the $11,000 alone. But the current benefit is just over $1,000 a month no matter how much the individual paid in taxes. We have no control over how much our money earns, who invests it, or even if we'll ever see it again. For taxpayers, this is one of the biggest pyramid scams around.

Nevertheless, despite all these facts, most people still expect to rely upon Social Security to finance a large portion of their retirement. As if you didn't need any more incentive to save and invest on your own, here are a few more:

- **The Pension Rights Center in Washington found that 60 percent of American workers don't even have a pension and that the 90 percent of Americans who don't save adequately for retirement will be forced into dependency upon friends, family, and government. Only one out of every ten Americans is prepared for retirement, according to the U.S. Census Bureau.**
- **The cost of living is still going up, even though our incomes may not be keeping pace. Although median incomes have**

tripled since 1970, Americans are saving only around 5 percent a year (not including Social Security, which is not a true savings plan). Developing countries like China and Korea are handily saving in the double digits.

- An estimated 46 percent of Americans are not participating in company-sponsored retirement plans. If they are offered the plans, only 25 percent participate, according to a study by Arthur D. Little and the WEFA Group. Of those who participate, the majority invest in fixed-income vehicles (for meager returns).

- Despite the explosion in mutual funds—now a $2 trillion–plus industry—only 21 percent of those assets are in stock retirement accounts, according to the Investment Company Institute.

- Americans who are saving and investing are doing it so conservatively, they fail to beat inflation. Ultrasafe U.S. Treasury bills, the investment of choice for most insured savings vehicles, averaged about 3.7 percent over the last sixty years. Ibbotson Associates found that you could do slightly better in intermediate U.S. bonds, which averaged 5.1 percent. But to really beat inflation and build a nest egg, you could more than double those returns with common stocks (in the S&P 500 index) at 10.4 percent and small-company stocks at 12 percent.

- Too many believe that past performance equals future gains. In print ads, mutual funds with monster gains began selling the ultimate big lie in investing: last year's performance. The truth—now trumpeted in fund ads under the caveat "Past performance does not guarantee future results"—is that in the year following a fund's best year, the same funds couldn't match the previous year's record. In fact, according to *Morningstar Investor*, while the first year of these top funds averaged a stunning 53.16 percent gain from 1987 to 1992, the second year showed a 17.10 percent uptick. The most volatile funds (typically technology) even lost money.

- At this writing, the mutual fund industry is a $2 trillion–plus business and is expected to surpass all the money held in banks and savings and loans within the next two years. Moreover, there are more mutual funds (four thousand and counting) than stocks on the New York Stock Exchange. Yet the majority of Americans investing in these investments— 56 percent—don't know that they're *not* insured by the government, much less how risky they are. Were these same people chastened after stock prices (and mutual funds) crashed in 1987? Or did they keep investing based on the glowing ads in their bank lobby?

As Joe Dominguez and Vicki Robin observe in their sagacious book *Your Money or Your Life* (Penguin, 1993), we work harder so that we can buy more.

Conditions have changed, but we are still operating financially by the rules established during the Industrial Revolution—rules based on creating more material possessions. But our high standard of living has not led to a high quality of life—for us or the planet. . . . What we need now is a new financial road map that is based on current global conditions and offers us a way out.

There is a way out. It involves a little education, persistence, and discipline. It's like learning to play the piano. At first it's dreadful because you're learning a new language and everything's foreign. Then you look for any reason not to practice. But after you hear your first legato melody or your first Bach prelude reveal its divine mysteries, the rest is a lifelong journey of exploration and reward. Learning how to invest will take some time, but it will pay dividends when you need them most.

The key fact to understand about investing is that the long-range history of the stock market is up (see chart). There are years when it dips a little, but it seems to bounce back—and move higher. How you invest in stocks requires some discipline and knowledge. So if you have a long-term approach, the stock market is not risky. History says you'll always come out on top—eventually. You risk far more, however, by doing nothing.

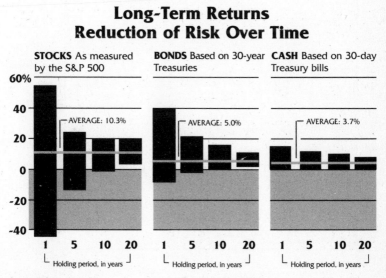

## Long-Term Returns
## Reduction of Risk Over Time

Source: Ibbotson Associates
Range of returns from 1926 through 1993, based on various indexes, with income reinvested.

Investfact: The Social Security Old Age and Survivors'
Trust Fund is expected to run out of money by 2029,
according to the U.S. Department of Health and Human
Services. Social Security's Medicare fund is expected to
run dry in 2001.

## Long-Range History of Stock Prices

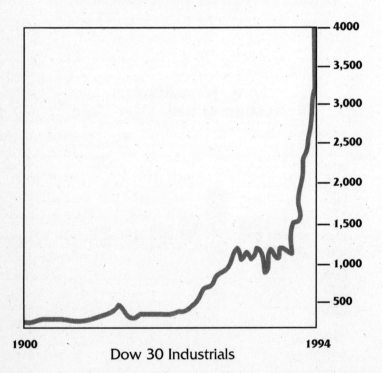

Dow 30 Industrials

## CHAPTER 3

# How Investment Clubs Do Better

If Social Security and company pension plans won't support you in your old age, what will? The old "three-legged" stool that has served as a metaphor for retirement investing has only one good leg to stand on, and that's yours. Millions are beginning to realize this—especially those who are looking at retirement within the next ten to twenty years. Some seventy-seven million "baby boomers" are spearheading the move for higher retirement investing returns. They were spurred along by 3.5 percent savings account yields, a slackening of inflation that no longer guaranteed that their homes would be retirement accounts, and the ongoing crisis over Social Security. To no one's surprise, a Merrill Lynch survey found that 85 *percent* of baby boomers don't expect Social Security to be a prime source of retirement income.

Millions have turned to the stock market. The explosion in mutual funds has occurred in tandem with the move to self-investing through individual ownership and investment clubs. Membership in the NAIC alone grew from 154,000 in June 1992 to more than 230,000 in June 1995. In the same period, inquiries to the group skyrocketed from 2,500 per month to 7,500 per month. That's an increase of 66 percent during a time in which the stock market took a bit of a powder.

Successful stock market investing *is* possible. Following the rules of fundamental investing can lead to an accumulation of millions. According to the NAIC's records, the thirteen $1 million–plus investors (their portfolios actually averaged $2 million) who have volunteered information on themselves have a few things in common:

- *They saved and invested over long periods of time.* Although small sums are suggested (ten dollars a month seems like a rock-bottom minimum), there is no limit. You must save, in order to invest. As the stock market rises and falls over time, regular investing takes advantage of "dollar-cost averaging." You lower your acquisition costs by buying throughout high and low price ranges. That's so that all your money doesn't come in at the wrong time. The average time the person had invested in stocks was 25.8 years.
- *They did their homework and reinvested dividends and gains.* To quote Albert Einstein, "The best invention in the history of mankind is compound interest." You learn that by pooling your dividend checks and profits, you compound your wealth over time. Money reinvested compounds. The greater the return, the greater the compounding. Nine out of the thirteen members used dividend reinvestment plans (DRPs) that allowed them not only automatically to reinvest dividends, but also to buy more shares without costly brokerage fees (more on DRPs on page 161).
- *They pooled their knowledge and invested in conservative*

*stocks that grew substantially over time.* In other words, they bought low, held long, and didn't sell very often. What is substantial growth? A common goal is a stock that doubles in five years or grows at 14.4 percent a year. Of course, it takes some careful research to find gems like these. The main thing is to beat inflation handily so that your investment is truly growing. What did they invest in? Many stocks were household names. Popular choices included AT&T, General Electric, Johnson & Johnson, Eli Lilly, Merck, Chrysler, Exxon, Eastman Kodak, Motorola, Chevron, Unilever, The Limited, Bristol-Myers Squibb, Heinz, Quaker Oats, Abbott Labs, Microsoft, and Philip Morris. They even won big on lesser-known companies such as Boatmen's Bankshares, HON Industries, NBD, American Power Conversion, Mylan Labs, Silicon Graphics, and Southtrust.

Imagine an average 13.9 percent a year, which is what most NAIC-member clubs did in 1993. You can actually do much better. Some of the better clubs have had years in which their portfolio rose 49 percent or more. And that's without brokers, accountants, or portfolio managers giving them an ounce of advice. They bought wisely and held.

Investfact: Of the more than 50,000 investment clubs in the United States, some 25 percent belong to the NAIC, averaging seventeen members apiece. The average club is 9.25 years old.

## INDIVIDUAL INVESTORS ARE GOOD
## FOR COMPANIES

Hopeful investors have come out on a steamy June night to the
Midway Motor Lodge, a hotel off Interstate 94 on the outskirts of
Milwaukee in Brookfield, Wisconsin. The highway links Minneapolis, Milwaukee, Chicago, Gary, and Detroit, representing a
thread in the web of the heartland. Along the route, Americans
make Harley-Davidsons and Fords, the steel that goes into them,
and thousands of other lesser-known products that are still the
backbone of American manufacturing. This is the America few
investors acknowledge, many write off, and only a handful
believe exists anymore. To the east of the hotel, the Milwaukee
Brewers play baseball in County Stadium. The jolly beer stein in
center field is witness to a working town of factories, breweries,
and conglomerates. They also love their baseball here. The *de
facto* commissioner of the game is Bud Selig, the car dealer who
owns the Brewers. The faithful who toil in manufacturing plants
by day want a good ball game at night and on weekends in the
too brief Wisconsin summer.

Lately, though, they've been more concerned about their own
financial futures than America's pastime. They want to know how
to beat paltry interest rates and the increasingly empty promise of
Social Security.

The small meeting room is nearly full. It's ninety-five degrees
outside and as humid as New Orleans, but there's no air-condi-
tioning on in the room. The program begins with display charts
on long-term stock investing. The numbers keep looking better
the longer one invests. African Americans, Asian Americans, and
middle-aged whites sit patiently to hear Milwaukee Council vol-

unteers talk about stock investing, dividend reinvestment, and setting up clubs.

Investors shuffle past NAIC volunteer Lorrie Guston at the room's reception desk. In the unglamorous, can-do world of the NAIC, she's one of the leaders, having helped hundreds of clubs form and profit. She has served as an officer on NAIC councils and boards, and she's also secretary of the World Federation of Investment Clubs, which will meet in Austria two weeks after this meeting.

Unlike most investment club members, who run their stock selection guides and comparisons in the relative calm of other people's living rooms, Lorrie has stepped beyond the role of mere investor. She's entered the corporate boardroom on an equal footing with the captains of industry.

One of her first contacts with the world of dark paneling and long tables came at an NAIC investor fair, which is a larger and more gregarious version of the introductory meeting she helped organize outside of Milwaukee. It was 1974, in the midst of a dark age for stock investors. Inflation was mushrooming, the stock market plummeting, and gasoline "shortages" creating long lines at the pump. Lorrie was eyeing booths of companies in an exhibition area. She noticed that RPM, a small, Ohio-based coatings company, was setting up. She remarked to the group of men clad in suits that it was "about time" they exhibited at an NAIC event, haranguing them playfully on the importance of courting amateur investors. She later found out that one of the "suits" was Tom Sullivan, president of RPM, a company that would eventually become a fixture on the investment club circuit.

RPM impressed Lorrie and her fellow club members. Not only did her clubs (she's been a member of eight) buy the stock over the years, but individual members bought it for their own portfolios. It was hard to resist. A long string of double-digit earnings growth, steady dividend increases, and a dividend reinvestment plan made it even more attractive (more on that later).

In the intervening years, RPM became a darling among NAIC members. Lorrie took up her place as resident counselor to clubs old and new, and the stock market continued its upward trek. But she didn't expect anything from companies like RPM except for an honest presentation at investor fairs. One of the reasons she was involved in clubs in the first place was that her (now-ex) husband had requested she learn investing while he started and ran an insurance business in the mid-1960s. She's since started and run two businesses of her own.

"All of us were looking for security beyond Social Security," she said of her club activities. "The ones who put effort into it got the most out of it."

As with most individual investors, "everything [stocks] I bought went down first" but later rose dramatically over time. Her thirty-three-year membership in the "Ticker Tape Tamales" club is evidence of her—and the NAIC's—buy-and-hold success. Several of their positions have climbed 50 percent in four years. Big winners have included (in addition to RPM) Worthington and AFLAC.

Boxes of candy also arrived every year from RPM's Sullivan— mostly tokens of friendship. Lorrie never really attached much significance to the gesture until last year, when Tom Sullivan asked *her* to serve on the company's board of directors. Although he was pressured to add an "outside" woman director, he told her how impressed he was with her knowledge of investing and thought she represented the "attitude" of the amateur investor. That is, she epitomized the kind of investor who invests loyally every month for twenty years and rarely sells. The kind of investor who sticks with a valuable concern and demands competent management. She accepted the offer and now serves on the audit committee, which monitors the company's financial statements.

Although it never made the front page of *The Wall Street Journal*, Lorrie's appointment as corporate director was a victory for amateur investors everywhere. To acknowledge that someone without an Ivy League or pin-striped pedigree was good enough for a major corporate governing body was a skyrocket announcing the growing power, influence, and success of small investors. The "attitudes" of small investors are changing the way global corporations do business. The price for their fidelity is progressive management and steady earnings and dividend growth. The reward to the companies: an intelligent group of investors who won't sell (and trash the stock price) unless management disappoints them. (The NAIC's Ken Janke is also a board director—for the AFLAC Corporation.)

Never has there been a more faithful symbiotic relationship in all of commerce. It grew up in living rooms from Seattle to Miami. Lorrie Guston and her Ticker Tape Tamales embody this pioneering spirit. Like her, the Tamales were working women from the Milwaukee area. Investment clubs work because they blend optimistic capitalism with the Puritan work ethic.

Will Rogers echoed the sentiments of millions when he gave his rule for investing in the stock market: "I only buy if it goes up; if it don't go up, I don't buy it." In a country where most investment is short term and often short-circuits when short-term gains don't materialize, Lorrie's brand of investing is restoring a sense of self-worth to those who wisely choose to ignore "sure things," dire headlines, daily stock prices, and lotteries. They do careful but dull analyses, inevitably lose some money along the way, but amass millions in the long term.

# PART II

## Setting Up a Club

# CHAPTER 4

## The Mother of All Investment Clubs

When Tom O'Hara was in high school, owning stock was a bit of an obsession. He talked to a friend about it but just couldn't get into the market the way he wanted to. There had to be a better way to profit than to look up a stock in the paper and buy it. In downtown Detroit there were two men who felt the same way Tom did, only they were a little farther along on how to buy stocks and eventually make a profit.

George Nicholson was a broker and an intellectual who was a student of the history of investment and capitalism. He knew how to find good companies, and he shared his knowledge with his secretary, Fred Russell. The year was 1940. Hitler had appropriated Austria and Czechoslovakia and cut a swath through Poland. On the other side of the world, the Japanese were brutalizing Asia and hunting for new sources of petroleum to keep their martial machine running. Most of the civilized world seemed to know what was coming next, yet they dug in for a massive denial. This was not a time when most people were thinking about long-term investing.

But in February of that year, Nicholson saw the merits of a club that would invest in the stock of American companies. These investments, chosen prudently using a set of simple mathematical tools, grew steadily over the years. Only a few breaths away from the Great Depression, most God-fearing Americans thought this idea sounded like nonsense. Nicholson, though, had seen stock clubs work well in Boston, so he wanted to give them a go in the Midwest.

When the attack on Pearl Harbor jolted America into the war, investing long term in anything but war matériel seemed like a sucker's game. After all, the great American industrial machine was gearing up to fight another world war. There were no televisions, no VCRs, no personal computers, and no automated teller machines. There was little in the way of material things that one could invest in anyway. Gasoline was rationed, and ladies' nylons became an incredible luxury.

Fred Russell got together with Nicholson, O'Hara, and some fraternity brothers at Wayne State University to form a club—an investment club. Nicholson, at thirty-two, was too old to be drafted. And Russell couldn't serve because of a heart problem. But O'Hara was shipped off to the army, still clinging to the idea of stock investments. Like a million other young men, he also wanted a future in which to invest.

Despite the war, Nicholson, Russell, and O'Hara kept in touch. O'Hara's correspondence proved to be so popular with army censors reading his mail that they would contact him for more stock tips. At the end of the war, his club had twelve members and $4,000 to $5,000 invested. At this point, though, he mostly saw investment clubbing as an educational venue and wanted to spread the word of the stock market's rewards to postwar America.

Ken Thompson of the *Detroit Free Press* thought he had a real scoop when he profiled O'Hara's club in 1949 with the headline 12 YOUNG MEN HAVE A GREAT SUCCESS WITH ORIGINAL IDEA. The article produced an astounding response of six hundred letters from readers who said the idea wasn't the least bit original because *they* were already in investment clubs. In fact, about half said they pulled out because they lost money. The other half stayed in because it was profitable. Apparently those who lost their shirts simply looked up stocks in the paper and bought at random. The successful investors, however, picked stocks using a fundamental method that's been proven to work over time.

Although he had a secure job at the Detroit Board of Education, in 1951 O'Hara quit his position to become chairman of the NAIC, the nonprofit trusteeship that advises and coordinates investment club activities throughout the United States. With Nicholson as its principal adviser and guiding light, investment clubs started out modestly through co-sponsored programs with the New York Stock Exchange.

Ken Janke, the first president of the NAIC, came aboard in 1960 after three years with Household Finance. Some 250,000 members, 14,000 clubs, and 57 regional councils later, the NAIC can claim that it's educated more amateurs about the stock market than any other nonacademic entity.

---

Investfact: In a survey of NAIC members conducted by *Better Investing*, some 37.9 percent said they had been common stock investors for five years or less. Some 21 percent said they had been stock investors for six to ten years. About 15 percent said they had been investing for twenty-one or more years.

---

# Number of American Shareowners

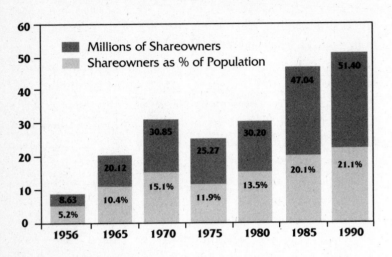

Figures from NYSE

## GETTING ORGANIZED

A group setting turns the whole affair of learning something new into a social event. You're also exposed to different opinions and ways of doing things. In investment clubs, there's also strength in numbers. You're pooling your money with others so that you don't have to risk as much of your own.

1. *Do you want to be in a club?* It's okay if you don't want to join a club. In fact, I joined the NAIC just for the informational materials and low-cost stock purchase plan (and that was before I even knew I would be writing a book about clubs).

Ironically, since I started my research, my wife has started a club for our extended family. You have the option of being your own investment club or including just a spouse or loved one. Some people just don't work well with others. Remember that this is as much a social activity as an educational and financial venture. If you feel confident investing on your own, check out the benefits of the American Association of Individual Investors in the resources section.

2. *Where can you find members?* Once you decide you want to be involved with others, talk to your friends, neighbors, church/temple members, co-workers, fraternal clubs, or family. Many clubs have some sort of affiliation before they start.

3. *Should you let in everyone who wants to join?* When your core group of up to twenty is together, do a survey among the members. Ask them if they are committed to learning about stock investing and willing to do some work toward that end. Then you need to know if anyone is not committed to a long-term horizon of more than five years. Since most clubs may lose money in their first years, this is a crucial question. If you obtain consensus on these items, you can move on.

4. *Your first meeting should be informal.* Discuss the shared goals, operation, and workload of the new club. Set a date for a follow-up meeting to allow everyone some time to think over what's involved. Everyone must be clear on the point that if they *all* don't contribute their time and research, the club won't work.

5. *The agenda of the next meeting covers ground rules for the club's operating procedures.* By this time you should have agreement on partnership papers and everyone should be familiar with how NAIC clubs operate.

6. *Once everyone understands the partnership agreement*—and

how profits/losses are either reinvested or divided — it's time to elect officers and set regular monthly meeting dates.

7. *Each member should know his or her responsibilities.* Most clubs assign individual stocks to members for study and analysis, which may take a few hours per week. A club's success or failure hinges on the willingness and quality of each member's work, so this requirement should be understood by everyone.

8. *Establish a set monthly amount that each member must contribute.* Most clubs start with ten to twenty-five dollars a month, although it can be more if all agree.

9. *Select a broker* (see section on selecting brokers in chapter 5). Although it's useful to have a broker who's dealt with clubs before, it's important that the broker thoroughly understand and accept the club's goals.

10. *Constantly update the club's knowledge base* by obtaining, analyzing, and discussing new sources of investment information. It's a good idea if members start clipping files on companies they are studying or have selected. The more information you obtain, the more you can share. It makes for better decision making.

## SETTING UP THE PARTNERSHIP

A partnership is the most popular structure chosen by investment clubs. Your other choice is a corporation, which involves more paperwork, legal work, and taxation. Unlike corporations, which must pay corporate income tax and pay taxable dividends, partnerships pay untaxed earnings directly to partners, where proceeds are taxed only once—at the individual level. Losses can also be passed through if capital losses are realized on trades.

Setting up partnerships is also a lot simpler than setting up a corporation. There are simply less filing requirements, although clubs must register their names with county clerks and pay a nominal fee. The partnership agreement should be inspected by a lawyer, although you—and your club members—should specify and review all of the language in it. It may seem amazing in this litigious age, but most partnership agreements can be written in plain English, so that everybody can understand them. In fact, every club member *must* understand the agreement thoroughly before it's signed.

The partnership agreement essentially outlines what the club may or may not do. For example, it may appoint certain "agents" (specific members) to represent the club to brokers or to keep the books. These sections on assigning responsibility are critical. Most clubs also elect a "presiding partner" who is like a president and organizes meetings. A "financial partner" should monitor all club purchases, expenses, disbursements, and trades. This partner is also responsible for drawing up a statement showing all of the club's portfolio activity, member contributions, and withdrawals.

You'll also need a "recording partner," who keeps and publishes minutes. Thorough and organized record keeping is crucial to a club's success.

Your club will thrive if it establishes bylaws and sticks to them. This club "constitution" can be customized to meet the needs of the club and can be amended from time to time. The NAIC provides model bylaws.

Partners also need to decide what kind of relationship they want with brokers and advisers. When you buy stocks, for example, do you want them held in the broker's "street" name (unless held in a dividend reinvestment plan) or have certificates issued? The former is most convenient in terms of bookkeeping. This way the broker holds the shares and pays dividends directly to the club's account. If the club chooses to hold shares directly, then dividends and splits are paid in the form of separate transactions.

There's also the problem of holding the shares (if you choose to take possession). You'll need to record the shares' CUSIP numbers and rent a safety-deposit box. Every time you add or sell shares, somebody will have to run to the bank. When shares are held in street names, transactions can be done by phone. Generally, one club member is authorized under the partnership agreement to deal with the broker. If you've chosen a full-service broker, however, you should invite the broker to one meeting for questions and presentations on stocks. That way, any member can ask a question in a public forum.

You also need to provide for how a member leaves the club. It's a fact of life: members need their money, move away, or die. That often puts clubs in difficult positions because they may be fully invested in the market and keep relatively small amounts of cash in the money market fund. So positions that have taken years to build—or new stakes that need time to grow—may get sacrificed.

Mary Jane A'Hearn, president of the Women's Investing Club (WIC) of Cincinnati, Ohio, said her club had a member who resigned, forcing the club to pay her off by redeeming the amount of shares equal to the number of units she owned (clubs determine ownership through units owned as a percentage of funds individually invested). As is typical with many clubs, they charged her a 2 percent redemption fee in accordance with their bylaws. Such events can't be avoided.

Your partnership agreement should also state:

1. how members may withdraw money (and if there's a withdrawal penalty before a certain holding period)
2. the authority of each partner (research, bookkeeping, recording minutes)
3. what happens if a member leaves a club or dies
4. limiting authority of members (which, if any, members may act in the partnership's interest without permission from other partners) and
5. provisions for regular meetings, reports (monthly/quarterly/annual).

Remember, the partnership agreement is a flexible document (before it's signed). You can write into it anything you want. In most active clubs, it's a good idea to rotate members in and out of positions, although certain members will be better at keeping books and organizing meetings.

## SAMPLE PARTNERSHIP AGREEMENT

Thanks to the Mutual Investment Club of Detroit, we have a working model for a club partnership agreement. Although you can make as many rules as you want in your partnership, the Mutual's agreement is a good starting point. It seems to have worked well for them. This is a summary of the club's agreement, first drafted and signed on February 1, 1940.

### Membership Agreement of (your club's name here)

This Agreement of Partnership, made as of (date here), by and between the undersigned (names of all partners).

**Formation of Partnership:** Must be in accordance with your state laws.

**Name of Partnership:** (your club's name here).

**Term:** The partnership shall begin on . . . and continue until . . . and continue thereafter from year to year unless earlier terminated as hereinafter provided.

**Purpose:** To invest the assets of the partnership solely in stocks, bonds, and securities for the education and benefit of the partners.

**Meetings:** Periodic meetings shall be held as determined by the partners (usually monthly).

**Contributions:** The partners may make contributions to the partnership on the date of each periodic meeting, in such amounts as the partnership shall determine, provided, however, that no partner's capital account shall exceed 20% of the capital accounts of the other partners.

*Note: This is flexible, meaning that clubs can prevent any one member from owning more than a fixed percentage.*

**Valuation:** The current value of the assets and property of the partnership, less the current value of the debts and liabilities of the partnership (herein referred to as the "value" of the partnership), shall be determined ten (10) business days preceding the date of each periodic meeting. The aforementioned date of valuation shall hereinafter be referred to as "valuation date."

**Capital Accounts:** There shall be maintained in the name of each partner, a capital account. Any increase or decrease in the value of the partnership on any valuation date shall be credited or debited, respectively, to each partner's capital account in proportion to the value of each partner's capital account on said date.

**Management:** Each partner shall participate in the management and conduct of the affairs of the partnership in proportion to his/her capital account.

**Sharing Profits and Losses:** Net profits and losses of the partnership shall inure to, and be borne by, the partners in proportion to the valuation adjusted credit balances in their capital accounts or in proportion to valuation unit balances.

*Note: This clause just says that profits and losses are to be borne by members proportional to how much they own, usually defined as "units."*

**Books of Account:** Shall be kept at all times and be available and open to inspection and examination by any partner.

**Annual Accounting:** Each calendar year, a full and complete account of the condition of the partnership shall be made to the partners.

**Bank Account:** The partnership shall select a bank for the purpose of opening a partnership bank account. Funds deposited in said account shall be withdrawn by checks signed by either of (2) partners designated by the partnership.

*Note: You'll have to designate who you want to deal with the bank.*

**Broker Account:** The partnership may select a broker and enter into such agreements with the broker as required, for the purchase or sale of securities. All securities owned by the partnership shall be registered in the partnership name unless another name shall be designated by the partnership.

*Note: You'll also designate members who will deal with brokers. In the case of dividend reinvestment plans, you'll deal with a bank acting as a "transfer agent." The Mutual Club also forbids members from acting as the club's broker, thus avoiding a conflict of interest.*

**No Compensation:** No partner shall be compensated for services rendered to the partnership, except reimbursement for expenses.

**Additional Partners:** May be admitted at any time, upon the unanimous consent of all the partners in writing or at a meeting, so long as the number of partners does not exceed (your number here).

**Voluntary Termination:** The partnership may be dissolved by agreement of the partners whose capital accounts total a majority in amount of the capital accounts of all of the partners. Notice of said decision to dissolve the partnership shall be given to all of the partners. The partnership shall thereupon be terminated by the payment of all the debts and liabilities of the partnership and distribution of the remaining assets either in cash or in kind to the partners or their personal representatives in proportion to their capital valuation accounts.

**Withdrawal of a Partner:** Any partner may withdraw a part or all of his/her interest. He/she shall give notice in writing to the recording secretary (partner).

*Note: You can insert a provision enabling the other partners to "buy out" the partner who leaves the club.*

**Death or Incapacity of a Partner:** Receipt of such notice shall be treated as a withdrawal.

*Note: Again, you can be as flexible as you want. You can assign a "grace" period in the case of incapacity or any other restrictions you deem appropriate.*

**Purchase Price:** Upon the death, incapacity, or withdrawal of a partner, and the exercise of the option to purchase by the other partners, said other partners shall pay the withdrawing partner or his/her estate, a purchase price, when payment is made in cash, equal to 97% of his/her capital account or his/her capital account less the actual cost of selling sufficient securities to meet the withdrawal, whichever is the lesser amount.

*Note: A partner who dies or is permanently disabled doesn't receive a 100 percent withdrawal of his/her capital account in order to cover commissions and other fees needed to make the withdrawal. There's a lot of flexibility here on timing, partial liquidation, and payment in the form of securities. In effect, you can make full withdrawal penalties as steep as you want. Remember, depending on how long the member has been in the club, you'll probably have to liquidate some stock, which may trigger a capital loss.*

**Forbidden Acts:** No partner shall sell without the unanimous consent of the other partners all or part of his/her interest in the partnership to any other partner or other person; use the partnership name, credit, or property for other than partnership purposes; do any act detrimental to the interests of the partnership or which would make it impossible to carry on the business or affairs of the partnership.

This agreement of partnership is hereby declared and shall be binding upon the respective heirs, executors, administrators and personal representatives of the parties.

IN WITNESS WHEREOF, the parties have set their hands and seal the year and day first above written.

**Partners:** (names typed out)

**Signatures**

---

Investfact: Average monthly investment per NAIC member: $37.23.

---

**CLUB TIP**

For tax purposes, make sure your club has a tax identification number. You can get this from any IRS office, along with the required form SS-4. All of your brokers and bankers will need this number to identify your club.

# CHAPTER 5

# The Broker Relationship

There's a joke that travels around investment seminars. A Wall Street broker decides one day that he wants to leave Manhattan for good, so he heads west. On the road he decides he wants to do something completely different, something so far removed from the world of finance that it will be refreshing and invigorating. At the foot of the Rocky Mountains, he comes across a shepherd with his flock. He stops his car and decides that he wants to try shepherding. But, still a financial man, he wants to hedge his bets.

"I want to buy *one* sheep to see what it would be like to be a shepherd," he says to the puzzled but wily shepherd.

"Why would you wanna do that?"

"I need to change my life, and I've just decided this is what I want to try. So how much do you want for one lamb?"

"I tell you what, mister," the crusty old shepherd replied. "If I can guess what you do for a living, you pay whatever *I* want. If I guess wrong, you can have a lamb for free. But first, pick out the lamb you want from my herd."

After closing his eyes and pointing into the flock, the cocky New Yorker picked an animal.

"Mister, you've given yourself away. You're a stockbroker."

"Incredible! How did you ever guess?"

"Out of my flock of three hundred sheep, you picked the only dog."

The point of this parable is that a little research can go a long way. It's almost too easy to follow Peter Lynch's advice and trot out to the shopping mall to see who's doing a healthy business and picking a stock based on that, and it's also a no-brainer to walk into a McDonald's or Wendy's and make a decision just by sampling their service and product. It works on a basic level.

The ideal broker is like the ideal in-laws. You don't want them to meddle. And it's a big plus for them to be helpful at the right times. Most of us will need to find a broker who provides a maximum amount of services for the least amount of money and hassle. The important thing to know about brokers before you choose one is that they never lose in their financial relationships with customers. They make commissions when you buy and when you sell in a "round-trip" trade. So it really doesn't matter if they sell you a good vehicle or a bad one.

If you trade a lot, they make more money. If you buy a bunch of dogs, they make even more, because you're then likely to dump stocks left and right and buy more or constantly turn over your portfolio. If you're the nervous type who likes to trade a lot, you're not only reading the wrong book, you're the broker's ideal customer. There's plenty of bad advice out there. Fraudulent or poor advice costs investors an estimated $1 billion a year. A survey conducted by the North American Securities Administrators Association (NASAA) focused on investor complaints from 1989 to 1992 totaling losses of $218 million. Half of the complaints were against securities brokers, insurance agents, accountants, tax preparers, and real estate brokers.

Unsuitable advice, negligence, and misrepresentation of investment facts by broker/advisers is on the rise. In 1992 the National Association of Securities Dealers (NASD) reported a record number of arbitration cases involving registered representatives (stockbrokers and financial planners who are licensed to sell securities products). The number of cases rose 43 percent to 4,000 from 2,800 decisions in 1989.

There are more than four hundred thousand financial advisers/brokers in America today. But that doesn't include financial planners and insurance agents, who add up to an additional one million financial brokers. Although most people who advise us on our investments, personal finance, and taxes and insurance are reputable, an increasing number of unscrupulous operators are taking advantage of consumers who ask for their help. They work in banks, insurance companies, brokerage houses, and boiler rooms.

No federal or state laws exist to regulate the advice part of the business, only the sales part. Brokers are regulated by the National Association of Securities Dealers, which is a "self-regulated organization" loosely watched by the U.S. Securities and Exchange Commission (SEC). Only twenty-six states mandate that adviser firms—not individuals—even register with state agencies.

Of course, those who sell insurance, securities, and real estate (or are accountants or lawyers) must have licenses and pass tests. But none of these laws cover the sale of financial advice. Such flimsy regulation has spawned fraud and deception. If a professional advises on money management, he or she should register as an investment adviser with the SEC and adhere to the rules of the Investment Advisors Act of 1940 (although relatively few do).

Insurance agents must be licensed by the state or states in which they do business.

Generally, those who call themselves advisers or consultants are basically *brokers* in a banker's suit—or lawyers or insurance agents. The one exception is fee-only financial planners, who charge solely for their time and make no money from their recommendations. Commissioned professionals, however, make money on what you buy and sell—without any responsibility for the return of these investments. Have you ever heard of a stockbroker or insurance agent rebating a commission if the investment vehicle they sold you tanked?

Through self-investing, you have all the accountability. Your decisions aren't tainted by how much you'll make on commission by "churning" your own account with dubious stocks.

Granted, responsible brokers do exist, but they still live and die by their commission volume. If they don't *sell*, they're out of work. So quantity, not quality, is the name of the game. Would you hire a surgeon based on how *many* organs were removed when you were on the operating table? Unfortunately, when it comes to investing, many of us are fully anesthetized.

You, can, however, pick and monitor your own investments and easily outperform the professionals. The most untainted advice will come from doing it yourself. Nearly any investment can be bought on a no-load (see page 231) or discounted basis, thereby making you money, but saving you money in the process.

## FINDING THE RIGHT BROKER

It's not difficult to find good brokers, but you need to know how to employ them. How should you use a broker? This is a fairly straightforward decision.

You either want someone to use his/her firm's research facilities to locate suitable investments (that you or club will later vote
on), or you just want someone to execute trades and buy other
vehicles.

If you want the first, you should consider a full-service brokerage house. Household names in this area include Merrill Lynch,
Smith Barney Shearson, Paine-Webber, Prudential, and Kidder
Peabody. Full-service brokers provide "handholding services,"
researching the entire spectrum of securities and making recommendations based on that research. This is essentially what you're
paying for here with commissions. They also sell a broad range of
investments ranging from U.S. Treasury bills to variable life
insurance and annuities. While there's no evidence to suggest
that their chosen investments do any better than those of the average investor, you have access to "one-stop shopping." Most large
brokerage houses even provide retirement and estate planning.

Unfortunately, full-service firms tend to be on the high end
when it comes to commissions, although you'll find that these are
negotiable for good customers. They know that you can always go
to another broker. They make more money by keeping you
happy, even if that means matching a discount broker's rate.

If you don't need research and advice but, instead, someone to
execute trades, choose a discount broker. Keep in mind that in
addition to being a salesperson, a broker is a middleman. Brokers'
NASD licenses permit them to trade securities. To obtain this
license, they need to pass a six-hour, 250-question test. No college education or professional training is required, although the
best service-oriented brokers have a strong background and are
market savvy.

The most important distinction between full-service and discounters is the method of compensation. Full-service brokers

work largely on commission. If they don't trade for clients and drum up business, they don't eat.

Discount brokers typically receive a straight salary, with bonus schedules based on total sales volume. In contrast, full-service brokers must hustle to get business, often making up to 750 calls per week. Discounters wait for the customers to come to them. In most cases they aren't allowed to pitch you a single investment idea or even call you back, except to confirm a trade.

In order to understand the present state of the brokerage business—and how you can best benefit from it—a little history lesson is in order. When discounters like Charles Schwab first appeared on the scene some twenty years ago, they were the Rodney Dangerfields of the business. The floodgates were opened when the SEC nixed the fixed-commission system in 1975. Since all the discounters did was execute trades, the big brokerages felt they had little to worry about and continued business as usual. Then the mutual fund industry and stock market boomed in the 1980s, bringing along millions of individual investors who had never invested in the stock market in their lives. Simultaneously, the investment information business exploded.

Software programs also made it easy for individuals to analyze, track, and trade securities on a home computer. Hundreds of newsletters and magazines emerged to cater to this new kind of investor—the do-it-yourselfer. This new breed of money manager didn't need or use the big firms on Wall Street. They bought no-load (no sales charge) mutual funds directly from mutual fund "families" (who also got into the brokerage business). And they didn't really need the kind of coddling offered by the full-service houses because they were doing their own research, much the way most investment clubs operate.

As if this trend weren't enough to alarm the cigar chompers on

Wall Street, what happened next made them drop their martinis altogether. For the stock market, 1987 was shaping up to be a record year. The Dow Jones averages were hitting new highs every day. Billions were flowing into the market as frustrated savings moved out of government-insured investment vehicles into the "can't miss" bull market that started around 1982. The lion's share of this new money came in about August 1987, when the market peaked for that year.

Few outside of Washington paid attention to James Baker, then secretary of the Treasury, when he made a reference to boosting the value of the dollar on foreign exchanges. But everyone on the Tokyo, London, New York, and Chicago markets took this as a signal that U.S. interest rates were going to rise, something both unwanted and unanticipated in the stock and bond markets. Or so one story goes.

All of the stock, bond, futures, and options markets posted the largest percentage losses in history on "Black Friday" and "Black Monday" in October of that year. Since few had ever experienced a crash in their lives, almost no one on Wall Street— except for the computers automatically triggering sell orders— were prepared for the debacle that followed. Some firms and investors were ruined. In fact, they were more than ruined: because of high leveraging (buying on credit), they lost more than they had invested by factors of ten.

Although mutual fund toll-free lines were jammed and fund investors also lost billions (on paper), the real carnage hit the full-service brokers. Unlike mutual fund and discount brokers, whose clients make their own investment selections, full-service brokers had themselves made picks for their clients that had bombed. They were the responsible parties in the eyes of many investors. They represented the Wall Street "old boy network" that fleeced their portfolios. Although no one knows for certain what caused the crash, it propelled a new wave of investors into the "do-it-yourself" market. This movement made discounters and mutual fund houses blossom.

## DISCOUNT BROKERS

Gone are the days when discounters simply executed trades for the lowest commission. Now there are discounters and "deep discounters" like Brown and Kennedy Cabot. If you do a volume trade, have a computer, or have a high net worth, you can save even more. Even the main-line discounters like Schwab and Quick & Reilly provide more service than the average bank does today.

The main difference between the deep discounters and the main-line discounters is the level of service. Deep discounters will trade your securities at the lowest possible cost, depending upon the number of shares traded and the price per share. Discounters, which provide a wide array of other services, have higher rates to pay for the cost of these amenities.

Discounters have diversified to capture even more business from mutual funds and full-service houses. Some firms even provide "personal representatives" to service your account. Here is a summary of services offered by discounters:

• *Consolidated statements.* These record-keeping devices combine all of your investments (funds, stocks, bonds, checking) onto one statement. This is a godsend at tax time.

• *Asset management accounts.* Although pioneered by full-service houses, the lowest fees on these accounts are offered through the discounters. Essentially this is an "all-in-one" account that combines brokerage, funds purchases, credit/debit cards, checking, and consolidated statements in one package. The most important feature "sweeps" money from securities sales directly into a money-market fund that's also attached to the account. This is a real time- and money-saving device. This will essentially be the main vehicle for your club's or personal account.

• *Mutual fund networks.* Again, this is another all-in-one service, though each discounter's offerings vary widely. For example, Schwab's "OneSource" offers you access to more than eight hundred mutual funds. They charge a commission of 0.6 percent of principal and a transaction fee of $29 to trade into one of the funds (subject to change). Also offered to a smaller degree by Jack White & Co., Fidelity Funds Network, and Quick & Reilly, this service saves you the time and paperwork in contacting individual funds. You're paying for the convenience, of course. But if you want a broad selection of funds and already have a brokerage account, this can be a timesaver when it comes to record keeping. Those 1099 forms have a habit of not appearing at tax time when you need them (see "Mutual Fund Services" in the resources section at the back of this book).

• *Some research material.* Although they don't tout stock picks or research, the discounters provide independent research reports from Standard & Poor's, Moody's, and Morningstar.

• *Computerized investing.* Most discounters allow you to trade from your home computer, offering you an additional discount. This is a great feature that enables you to track your trades using quality portfolio management software. No paperwork is involved at all. Some, like Schwab, even provide software at an additional price. With the software you can manage, monitor, and trade your portfolio without leaving your computer. Just keep in mind that most on-line trading services carry additional "on-line" charges that you won't incur with a straight discounter. They are mainly for convenience.

• *Insurance products.* Discounters are often a less costly route to buying variable annuities and cash-value life products.

## SERVICES BROKERS OFFER

The modern brokerage house—whether a discounter or full service—provides an extensive product selection. Here's what brokers offer, no matter where you go:

- Stocks; corporate, municipal, zero-coupon, and U.S. Treasury bonds; mutual funds; unit investment trusts; options; futures; margin accounts; and record keeping.
- Variable annuities; life insurance; twenty-four-hour access to account balances; on-line computer trading and information; personal or "wrap account" (outside managers) money management; estate/retirement planning; investment software; "in-house" mutual funds; college financial planning; tax and accounting services; fee-only investment advice; securities research.

Most brokerage accounts also have "sweeps" features that automatically place uninvested funds into a money market fund. While these funds are hardly designed to enrich you, they do earn your money some interest while you or your club are deciding how to really put it to work.

If you're truly diligent—or your club is anxious about it—you can search for the highest-yielding money market mutual fund by poring over *Barron's, The Wall Street Journal,* or *Money* magazine. Money funds typically differ little in terms of real return (after inflation and management fees). If you're starting out, though, chances are you won't have enough of a balance (usually at least $1,000) to get into a money fund. In that case, find a no-fee checking account or a money fund attached to a brokerage account. But if you insist on chasing that extra yield, here's how to do it:

1. Search financial sections of newspapers for the highest-yield money funds (avoid banks because they typically don't pay as much as mutual funds).
2. Find funds that combine high yield with low or no management fees. Some of the highest-yielding funds actually waive their management fees.
3. Make sure that the fund(s) you choose will not pose a paperwork problem. This may be the most important factor because you'll need to write checks or transfer money into your brokerage account every time you buy or sell a security. Brokerage accounts that already have links to money funds don't have this problem. So if it's important to avoid the headache of two sets of records—just for monitoring your cash balances—stick with the brokerage account fund. Also keep in mind that if you start chasing the highest yield, you're trying to catch a chameleon. Rates change every day, and the "top ten" list changes with it.

## HOW TO CHOOSE A BROKER

This checklist will help you determine what your brokerage needs are. You should choose a half-dozen companies from the list at the end of this chapter and request their literature and commission schedules. After screening this information, complete the following checklist.

[  ] Do we need a full-service or discount brokerage? That is, do we need additional outside investment research? If so, choose a full-service house.

[  ] Do we need the lowest possible commissions? If so, choose a discounter.

[  ] Will we require additional services such as asset management accounts, insurance products, or mutual funds? If so, compare the offerings and prices of the top full-service and discounters.

[  ] Do we need a brokerage that provides on-line trading or software?

[  ] Do we need premier services such as twenty-four-hour access to our account?

[  ] If using a full-service broker, what is the broker's background in the business? Does he/she have additional skills or education that your club will find useful (tax planning, securities analysis)?

[  ] Will the (full-service) broker willingly provide background details about his/her professional record? That is, has the broker ever been sued, censured, or sanctioned by the NASD or SEC? Has the broker's securities license ever been suspended?

[  ] Check a broker's record. Call the NASD (800-289-9999).

[  ] Can your broker provide referrals of clients he/she's had for more than three years? (Ask of each full-service house.)

---

**CLUB TIP**

If you want to start out simple, though, buy a share through a low-cost program (see pages 170–74). That way you won't have to use a broker or pay a commission on a small number of shares.

---

## HOW TO NEGOTIATE COMMISSIONS

Most brokers are honest and will do everything they can to keep your business. Remember, we're in the age when financial consumers are calling the shots. The whole "no-load" and "discount" commission revolutions were launched because the government and the securities business realized that the industry would grow much faster if they pleased more individual investors. It's not in a broker's best interests to send you to the competition. They *can* price their services to get your business.

The most basic rule to remember is that you shouldn't pay too much for your brokerage services. Even more to the point, all commissions are *negotiable*. Even if the brokerage house publishes a schedule, you don't have to abide by it. In doing research for a financial planning piece, I had a chance to ask a major full-service broker what he thought if I wanted to take my trades to a deep-discount broker. "We'll match their commissions," he said plainly. And so will any broker who wants to keep your account.

Since the fixed-commission system went out the door in 1975, every commission is negotiable. That's why there's a discount brokerage industry and you can buy stocks through your bank, insurance, and mutual fund companies. Why pay top dollar on every transaction when you don't have to? If you wish, you can call a toll-free number and employ the best management through a no-load mutual fund. Brokers know this; they realize their business can disappear if they don't accommodate you with the best service and rates. Don't be afraid to negotiate. They are competing for your business, not the other way around.

Brokers bank on the fact that few investors know that commissions are negotiable. Most full-service firms simply redirect their high commissions back into salaries, bonuses, and research you may not even use. In his book *What Your Stockbroker Doesn't Want You to Know* (Business Publishing), Bruce Sankin notes that "your broker has the authority to offer you a 5 percent to 20 percent discount. However, most brokers will not volunteer this information, since it means that they will make less money from the trade. If you want the discount, you must ask the stockbroker for it."

As a broker himself, Sankin knows that discounts eat into commissions, but brokers' compensation packages are based on how much total business they generate for the firm. So it's reasonable to expect that if you get discounts, you'll want to do more business with a particular broker and not hit the bricks to find lower commissions. In this scenario, everybody wins.

If the broker resists giving you a commission, tell him/her to ask their manager to authorize lower rates. Sankin says that a 3 percent full-service trade is too much; 1 percent to 2 percent per transaction is more fair.

Another negotiation strategy is to ask for a *per share* rate. It's possible to obtain a $.10 to $.25 per share rate if you push—even less if you can get the broker to match a competing rate from a superdiscounter advertising in *Barron's* or *The Wall Street Journal*.

If they won't meet your price, it's a free market. Just keep in mind that every penny you pay in commissions takes away from what you can invest. If you pay $120 (3 percent commission) on one hundred shares of a $40 stock, your total invested amount is $3,800. On the same transaction—only with a 1 percent commission—your invested amount is $3,960. You not only save $80, you're able to invest it. Multiply that $80 savings over a few years' worth of trades, and you're looking at a significant savings. If you make twenty trades per year for five years, that's $8,000 ($80 savings per trade times one hundred total trades). That's half the price of a new subcompact car or a down payment on a modest home. And if it's well invested, all that money will be *compounding*.

Your club can negotiate discounts based on the volume of business you do. But don't expect big discounts if you have a small portfolio or buy only a few shares at a time. The discounts develop over time—but you have to ask for them.

## COST SAVERS YOUR BROKER WON'T MENTION

Now that you've learned that brokers are primarily salespeople (and that's not necessarily a bad thing by itself), here are other key points to remember:

• *Don't buy mutual funds through a broker.* They charge a commission on a product for which they provide little guidance. Most information on mutual funds is available directly through the fund managers or through mutual funds services like Morningstar or Value Line (see mutual fund and resources sections). Why pay for something and not get anything in return?

• *If you're buying a stock through a broker, ask if the firm is "making a market" for that stock.* Several brokerage houses develop markets for "initial public offerings," for example, by selling them aggressively. Of course, unless you're an institution or have a lot of money to invest, you're not going to get the best price. You'll get an inflated price that's likely to drop dramatically once the stock's initial public offering period is over. Some full-service brokers also push particular stocks harder than others because they receive better commissions for selling them. Market making is not a problem with discount brokers, however. Their commissions don't vary on the individual stock, only on the price and amount of shares.

• *Beware "free" research.* The only research that's free is research that has no strings attached. Brokerage houses and analysts don't always recommend stocks because they are good values for individual investors. They will give you old S&P books if you ask for them.

• *You're the buyer and shouldn't be "sold" on a stock.* This is a subtle but important distinction. Some stocks may be unsuitable for you or your club. That is, they may be too speculative, popular, or overpriced or may involve bad management.

• *Under no circumstances should you give your broker "discretionary" powers over your account.* That means they can trade at will, racking up commissions needlessly through abuses known as "churning."

## BAD BROKERS

Bad trades and brokers cost you money. But there's no reason to bite the bullet without compensation. Be properly prepared and aware of your rights should a dispute arise:

1. Keep and examine all your trading statements. Was the trade(s) authorized? When? By whom? Did you (or the

club's authorized agent) keep a record of when (and if) you made the call to transact a trade? Documentation is your best defense.

2. Call the broker and discuss it. If it was the broker's fault, and your records clearly show it, then you may be able to resolve the dispute at the company level. If your broker stonewalls you, talk to the office's manager. If no resolution is forthcoming, you have a right to arbitrate.

3. When you signed your account agreement, you essentially agreed to arbitrate any disputes according to rules set out by the NASD. This process is a legally binding decision-making procedure that avoids the court system. It's faster, cheaper, and less involved than filing suit. Of course, you can always find lawyers who specialize in securities arbitration, although the process is relatively simple and you can do it yourself. If a large sum of money is involved, however, you may want a lawyer to present your case. Just keep in mind that lawyers will charge you for their time or take a percentage of the recovered amount. For information on arbitration, ask your broker or write to the NASD at

> **NASD Financial Center**
> **33 Whitehall Street**
> **New York, NY 10004**
> **(212) 858-4000**

4. In preparing your case for arbitration, you need to prove that the trade was illicit in some way. Review all your account agreements, sale literature/prospectuses, commission statements, and any other material supplied by the broker. Witnesses are also important, especially if they can testify on your behalf. The arbitration hearing proceeds like a court

trial. There are witnesses, presentations, and cross-examinations. If your case is solid, you stand a good chance of receiving a fair settlement. A decision is usually delivered within thirty days of the hearing.

5. You can avoid lots of problems from the outset by identifying brokers who have bad records. The NASD now provides information on broker backgrounds (suits, regulatory sanctions, criminal actions, and so on) through their Central Registration Depository; call (800) 289-9999.

## THE BROKERAGE AGREEMENT

A good brokerage agreement merely outlines what you expect your broker to do. Do you want a margin account—the ability to borrow money to buy securities? Will you be trading options or futures? The agreement is essentially a contract (written in plain English) that spells out:

1. confidentiality
2. compensation
3. responsibilities (yours)
4. responsibilities (the broker's)
5. power to transfer funds or trade securities in your name (or the club's)
6. arbitration rights
7. margin, options, or commodities trading

All of the elements of the agreement—especially the fifth one—are subject to negotiation. It's a bad idea to give your broker power of attorney, unless you want to surrender control over your financial affairs. Another surefire tip: Avoid brokers who promise unusually high rates of return.

## BROKER SAFETY CHECKLIST

[ ] Check every confirmation statement. Was the trade authorized? Are the particulars (share price, number of shares) correct? If not, call the broker immediately. You have five business days before the trade is "settled."

[ ] Is your broker "churning" your account? That is, do you feel he/she is trading excessively to generate commissions? Remember, every trade must be authorized by you or another club member.

[ ] Did you buy/sell at a set price or "at market"? This should be noted on your statement. Buy/sell orders can be made for the day or indefinitely (whenever the desired price is reached on the open market).

## BROKER RESOURCES

### Broker Discount Surveys (lowest rates)

AAII (312-280-0170)
Mercer (800-582-9854)

### Major Full-Service Brokers

Dean Witter (800-869-3863)
Merrill Lynch (800-637-3863)
Paine Webber (800-617-1568)

Prudential Securities (800-225-1852)
Smith Barney Shearson (800-544-7835)

## Discounters

Fidelity/Spartan (800-544-9697)
Olde (800-872-6533)
Quick & Reilly (800-222-0437)
Schwab (800-526-8600)
Muriel Siebert (800-872-0444)
State Discount (800-222-5520)
Jack White (800-323-3263)

## Deep Discounters

Brown & Co. (800-822-2829)
Kennedy Cabot (800-252-0090)
Lombard (800-688-0882)
National Discount (800-417-7423)
T. Rowe Price (800-225-5132)
Waterhouse (800-934-4410)

## Computer Traders

Accutrade (800-762-5555; 800-544-4900)
America Online (800-827-6364)
CompuServe/QuickWay/E*Trade/Tickerscreen (800-848-8199;
   800-786-2573; 800-634-6214; 800-223-6642)
Fidelity Online Express/FOX (800-544-9375)
Prodigy/PCFN (800-776-3449; 800-825-5723)
Quick & Reilly (800-222-0437)
Schwab/Streetsmart (800-526-8600; 800-334-4455)

# CHAPTER 6

## Running a Club Smoothly

When you get right down to it, the dynamics of a successful investment club are pretty simple. Some people will exhibit leadership qualities and steer the club in some direction, and others will follow. Yet others will inevitably not be as ambitious as the leader. No matter what you do, however, you'll need patience and organization. Without it, nothing will get done and you'll lose money.

What successful clubs have in common are detail-oriented members who are devoted to their club duties. "It takes a strong leader who does a great deal of work to run a successful club," Tom O'Hara has found after more than fifty years of observing clubs. "It may be five to six years before you see results, so it also takes some diligent study [of quality stocks]."

Ted Crockett, the "presiding partner" of the "Money Uppers" club in Milwaukee, says his club has stayed together for twenty-five years as a result of discipline and following stock selection guidelines closely. Members of his club know that if they don't analyze the stock in some detail, they'll get "shot down" by other members.

"Each meeting we have a roll call where each member must

say whether the club must buy, sell, or hold the two stocks that they're assigned to monitor," Crockett says. To date, this routine has worked well for the club, which Crockett says has averaged 18 percent per year. Big winners in the twenty-two-stock portfolio include Pepsico, Hewlett-Packard, Seagate, Philip Morris, and Philadelphia Electric. No more than 5 percent of the club's portfolio is *speculative*. The last speculative stock they bought—JWP Inc.—went Chapter 11, though there have been other successes.

## TYPICAL CLUB MEETING AGENDA

1. President calls meeting to order.
2. Minutes presented, read, corrected (if necessary), and approved.
3. Old business (business from last meeting, unresolved matters) discussed.
4. Portfolio review (review and discussion of stocks within portfolio by each member assigned to follow stocks). For example, members can discuss earnings reports or changes in company management. Each holding should be reviewed each meeting, unless there's no news.
5. New business (new stocks presented for discussion, upcoming events, educational presentations, new on the market or portfolio holdings). The president can assign new stocks for review or discuss new developments.
6. Adjournment.

*Points of Discussion*: Are stocks performing up to expectations? Are there any events (bad earnings reports, and the like) that will require a club vote?

## COMMON QUESTIONS

The following are some questions and answers for novices based on the findings of my research:

• *How do I find a club to join?* Network, network, network. Since most clubs are fairly private affairs, you'll have to put the word out. Churches, fraternal groups, employee groups, and senior centers are good places to start. Some clubs make their meetings open to the public—and may even post a notice in a newsletter or newspaper. These clubs also usually have waiting lists and require you to wait several months (and attend meetings on a regular basis) before you can join. If all of these routes lead nowhere, start your own club. Remember, you only really need two persons to have a club, but you'll learn more if there are more. A diverse group of people you don't know that well also helps—as long as they have the desire to make a commitment to their financial education and participate in the work necessary to run the club. Although the NAIC suggests that fifteen members are an ideal size for a club, smaller groups may be more workable for many people.

• *How much do I need to invest?* Start out with $10 a month per member; you can raise the monthly contribution later. That amount is just a starter. You can contribute as much as you want in the future. The idea is, you're risking little and learning a lot. When can you raise the monthly minimum? When everyone is feeling comfortable about their skill level and wants to invest more. There really is no limit to the monthly minimum, although most clubs have bylaws forbidding ownership of more than 20 percent of club assets. Put it to a vote. Majority rules.

• *When can we start buying stocks?* When you've raised

enough cash to build a position in a particular stock or stocks. This, of course, depends upon the stocks you choose and the price you choose to buy at. It's a good idea to start small and through a dividend reinvestment plan keep your costs as low as possible. Low-cost purchase plans through the NAIC (see pages 172–73) and other groups are also good places to buy your first shares.

• *How long should the meeting last?* As a general rule, it's best to set a specific meeting time and duration. Otherwise the meeting will tend to ramble and you won't get anything done. Typically, meetings run from one to two hours. Vote on meeting times and stick to it. Examples include second Tuesdays of every month except for August and December. Several groups end their formal business and serve coffee and treats. Others have the meeting over dinner. It's up to you and your fellow members. Just keep in mind that you're primarily doing business first; socializing and eating are secondary.

• *How should the meeting begin?* Like most formal meetings, you need to take attendance and read the minutes of the last meeting. You should also present all minutes (typed and copied) and financial reports (club account statements and transactions) so that each member can review them at the beginning of the meeting. From there, you move on to old business (current positions/portfolio review and updates) and new business (proposed stock buys and future meeting topics/speakers). Before the meeting ends, make sure each member knows what he or she is responsible for (checking a stock, communicating with the broker, and so on) and when to report back to the group. All actions should be reflected in the minutes. Another sound strategy is to have an experienced investment club member attend your first few meetings and provide some pointers. Sticking to an agenda and starting on time will keep the meeting flowing.

• *How many officers should a club have?* Again, this is a matter you put to a vote. Generally, you need a presiding partner/president, assistant presiding partner/vice president, secretary (keeps track of all correspondence/records), recording partner/secretary (keeps minutes and distributes them), and financial partner/treasurer (works with broker, disburses funds, keeps all financial records). Some clubs have more officers depending upon the size of the club. But these are the core positions. Typically, you vote on these positions every year and can choose to rotate members into different positions when terms are up. There are, however, cases where certain members are particularly good at record keeping or keeping notes, so they can remain in their positions if they feel comfortable. The responsibilities of each member should be clearly written out and understood by each member. Also include all officers' duties in your club's bylaws.

• *How should we deal with the broker?* Your first decision is to decide which club member should be appointed to deal with the broker. Typically, the financial partner or secretary makes all trades—fully authorized by the club. Next you should decide what kind of broker to employ (see page 52). Full-service, discount, and deep discount are the choices.

• *How can we manage risk?* Diversify to insulate yourself against market risks. It also helps to ask yourself how much risk you want to take and what you want your portfolio to do, and set your goals and choose your risks accordingly. Do you want your portfolio to provide an early or comfortable retirement? Is it a college education fund? Is it just a supplement to your company pension plan and/or Social Security?

• *How do I know we're making good decisions?* Whether you

invest on your own or with a club, for a reality check, bounce your decisions off an informed person—somebody else who knows stock picking (but not a broker). Such people are especially valuable if they know fundamental analysis and are willing to be honest with you. Spouses, significant others, relatives, financial professionals, and others may qualify if they know what they're talking about—and have nothing to gain by their comments and advice.

## FIVE HABITS OF HIGHLY EFFECTIVE INVESTMENT CLUBS

1. Invest small amounts on a regular basis.
2. Pick quality growth companies using fundamental analysis of management, price, dividends, and related factors.
3. Reinvest your dividends and gains and look for opportunities to buy more when prices are right on quality stocks.
4. Be patient. You have a lot to learn, and it'll take several years before you're truly successful. Learn from your mistakes and stay the course. Even those who guess badly on the "right time" to buy stocks still make money over decades if they just stay in the market.
5. Enjoy yourself. This is a social as well as an educational venture.

## TROUBLESHOOTING

There are some definite signals that will tell you if things aren't working out. Fortunately there's something you can do about it to bring about a healthy group dynamic. There are a number of ways to stem major problems if they're discussed and resolved. The following tips are suggested by Ken Janke, president of the NAIC.

• *Failure is okay.* Yes, that's right. This is how we learn. The early NAIC members assumed that their first stock picks wouldn't make money. As we mentioned before, the NAIC tells its clubs not to expect any consistent, positive results until after at least five years of operation. Half of new clubs fail. But they can succeed if they decide to learn from their mistakes.

• *You have to risk your own money in order to learn more.* "Until you risk your funds, you're not going to learn," Janke has discovered. "Make your mistakes early on with small amounts of money—that way you'll have little money at risk." In other words, you will set yourself up for a fall if you start with large monthly investments.

• *If you're starting the club, don't do it only with people you know.* People often move more cautiously if there are strangers among the core group. Janke notes that only a small percentage of investment clubs are composed of families. Diversity of membership is desirable.

• *If you favor investments the club doesn't choose to exploit, don't feel excluded.* Pursue them on your own. Most club members invest on their own anyway.

• *One person should not dominate the club by calling all of the shots.* Clubs should be democracies.

• *Irreconcilable differences in investment philosophies can cause rifts.* Make sure all are in agreement as to the group's investment goals. If a member or two think that the group should buy options and the rest of the group disagrees, that could cause divisiveness. Make sure these possible conflicts are eliminated in your first few meetings. Write down your investment objectives. That documents the group's intentions.

- *The majority rules.* If there isn't general agreement, bring it to a vote. Majority rules. Defer to your bylaws and partnership agreement to settle disputes. If there isn't a rule covering your disagreement, make a new rule to avoid future disputes.

- *It's okay to speculate with small amounts of club funds (as long as everyone agrees and knows the risks).* Most clubs refer to this as "seat of your pants" picks. After running the basic analyses, if a member has a hunch, it may be worth exploring—if the rest of the club agrees to a small stake.

- *Remember that your club is an educational venture.* You're there to learn from others and yourself. It's also a social setting that allows discussion and insight. Don't be afraid to offer your ideas and arguments. Your experience forms a base for your personal portfolio.

- *If you're concerned about the integrity of your club's account, obtain insurance bonding.* Although it should be standard practice for the treasurer to present the most recent brokerage statement to all members at every meeting, bonding is a good way to protect against the unexpected. A bond, available through insurance companies, simply covers the club's assets if a member finds a way to abscond with the club's portfolio. Tom O'Hara, the NAIC's chairman, said he can't recall a problem of that nature within the last ten years, but he recommends bonding if the club feels nervous about it. The NAIC offers bonding to its members.

- *Present all statements to members upon request and perform quarterly or yearly audits.* This ensures that everybody knows how much cash is on hand, the state of the portfolio, and the transactions that've been made. Audits simply make sure that everything is square in the club's ledger.

• *Reread and update club bylaws periodically.* The bylaws are the club's constitution, and they must keep up with the needs of the membership. They can be updated to accommodate new requirements, but they need careful discussion. Most older clubs have guidelines on such issues as whether to charge membership fees, withdrawal charges for those who quit (or die), and limits on stock trading and individual ownership. The NAIC also provides model bylaws to members.

## ADVICE FROM AN EXPERT CLUBBER

There's nothing unusual about arguing at meetings, although it should be done in a tone of respectful discussion. The important thing to remember is that it's a meeting of interested parties. It's not fair if one member bullies others or tries to dominate. Not every club will succeed. Those that break up do so because they ignore a few basic rules.

When it comes to the ground rules on starting and running clubs—as well as personal investing—there are few brighter lights in the NAIC organization than Peggy Schmeltz, who resides in Bowling Green, Ohio. Peggy is one of the many reasons the NAIC doesn't have to pay to advertise. She's a dynamo who engenders word of mouth and seeds clubs wherever she goes.

A chairperson of the NAIC's board of directors, she has been president on the regional and club level. In addition to being an ace investor in her own right, she is a member of three clubs in northwest Ohio and has helped start more than one hundred others. Many of them began when she first started in the NAIC, lecturing at air force bases. She says she spends "from dawn until dusk researching stocks, with the rest of the time spent on the road as a volunteer lecturer in front of other clubs across the country."

Peggy's own seven-figure success has made her a bit of a folk hero within the NAIC. Her NAIC involvement—starting with the creation of the Northwest (Ohio) Buckeye Council—spans more than seventeen years and has paid for the college educations and home down payments of her four married children. Every Christmas she gives $1,500 worth of stock to her ten grandchildren for their college funds. She estimates that every grandchild has at least one year of college paid up. One fourteen-year-old grandson has $16,000 in his kitty.

Although her husband, Bill, is a former college dean, accountant, and financial analyst, her stock picks are all her own. She defers to him only on matters of corporate debt and cash flow. In between raising her children and investing, she's found time to obtain a master's in business, advise the New York Stock Exchange's Individual Investor Advisory Committee, train NAIC delegates, advise the NAIC growth fund, and lecture in thirty-five states.

Her three clubs—"First Ladies," "Mount Ararat," and "Signal Watchers"—are a testament to Peggy's discipline and energy. The Signal Watchers' portfolio alone is worth some $680,000 (at this writing) and makes decisions by mail since the forty members are so spread out. That club has nearly doubled its return on its initial investment. First Ladies has done well enough to be able to pay yearly special dividends from $500 to $1,000 from monthly contributions that started at $10 a month (it's now $30 a month). Mount Ararat has had similar success with its twenty members.

What's the central element in the success of these organizations?
Here are some keys to success she's gleaned from her experience:

- Keep in mind that "it takes a few years to get your portfolio
  going." You're going to have some losses at first, but hang in
  there.
- "If you have a good stock that goes lower—and all of the
  fundamentals are sound—have some confidence and buy
  more. It'll lower your average [purchase] cost."
- "Make sure your portfolio isn't loaded up with all cyclical
  stocks [see chapter 11, on business cycles]. Have some
  defensive stocks such as food and drugs."
- "Out of five stocks you select, one won't meet criteria [for
  profitability], three will be marginal or losers, and one will
  be a big winner that will take care of losers." She cites her
  purchase of Home Depot, which turned an initial $5,000
  investment into $190,000.
- "If you have a winner, don't be afraid to sell a portion of it
  or half. If profit or management conditions change, look for
  another stock to replace it." She managed to sell IBM at
  $138 a share. It peaked at $139 before its descent into the
  abyss of management turmoil and investor disfavor.
- Holding on to a good stock keeps rewarding you for just
  holding. Peggy says that Huntington Bank (Columbus,
  Ohio) and General Electric have been two of her biggest
  winners because of consistent stock splits. Every time a split
  takes place, you can lower your cost of acquisition.
- "Investing takes time and patience. If you wait long enough,
  you can get the right price. Look at a large number of
  stocks."
- The size of your club is important. Small clubs have less

money to invest and fewer ideas. "The more people involved, the more [variety of] judgment you'll have."

- Every member of a club must contribute. "Three or four members shouldn't be doing all of the work. There should be no silent partners. All must contribute. Everybody should do something. You should have members resign if they refuse to do anything."
- "Each member should monitor a different publication [see list in resources section at back of book]. And every member should be able to quote the positions in at least half of the portfolio."
- "Everybody should be familiar with the NAIC manual. Officers should read it on a regular basis."
- Use buying decisions within the club as a challenge to your own portfolio management skills. If a club buys a stock, "see if you can buy it lower [on your own] and double your money faster." This way, the club acts as an educational fulcrum to your own investing achievement.
- Spend at least one hour reviewing the club's portfolio every week.
- Try to read outside investment resources such as *Value Line* and share your insights with the club. Watch for and clip articles relating to stocks held or being considered.
- Plan to attend a seminar or workshop during the next year to broaden your investment skills.
- Offer to do stock reports and become better acquainted with other club members.

## ARE YOU A RESPONSIBLE CLUB INVESTOR?

To be considered a good club member, you should be able to answer at least 75 percent of the following questions, according to Peggy:

- If you were asked to name the companies your club has in its portfolio, how many could you name offhand? You should be able to name at least half.
- Could you figure out the approximate dividend yield on each of the stocks in your portfolio (within 1 percent)?
- Do you know how many different industries are in the portfolio? Are they in foods, drugs, technology, or consumer products?
- Can you say what stocks or industries your club has discussed in the last six months? Can you name five or six companies being studied?
- Do you know how much your club (or you) has available every month for investment? What is the value of your portfolio?
- When was your club organized? How many members are there? Can you name more than half of them?
- Do you know how much the club earned in dividends last year?
- Did you attend any (local NAIC) council meetings or other investment programs where you brought in information to be shared with the group?
- Have you offered to do a stock selection guide or give a report on a company or industry with another member for the purpose of self-improvement?
- Offhand, which of your stocks are the "big winners"? Which have done poorly? Which have split or paid dividends? Can you summarize what makes winners?

# PART III

# Building a Portfolio

Much of the NAIC's successful philosophy is reflected in the portfolio of the seminal Mutual Investment Club of Detroit (Mutual). Started in 1940, the club still counts not only O'Hara and Janke among its twenty-one members, but their sons as well. The club's portfolio exemplifies so many "buy and hold" success stories that it's a book in itself.

The Mutual portfolio is a Rosetta stone of typical club portfolios. It's loaded with quality, growth-oriented companies that keep on growing (although some companies have been troubled in recent years). There are dozens of huge winners in companies most investors take for granted or know nothing about. Following is just a sampling of positions in some key stocks, the biggest winners (not reflecting stock splits) of the thirty-eight-stock portfolio:

| Stock | Original Cost/Share | Price (as of mid-1995) |
| --- | --- | --- |
| AFLAC | $1 | $43 |
| Amoco | 20 | 66 |
| Colgate-Palmolive | 23 | 75 |
| Dow Chemical | 21 | 72 |
| Eastman Kodak | 23 | 62 |
| General Electric | 26 | 56 |
| Lawson Products | 5 | 26 |
| McDonald's | 26 | 38 |
| Mobil | 14 | 98 |
| NBD Corporation | 3 | 32 |
| Pentair | 7 | 43 |
| Sears | 14 | 59 |

You may notice that most of these stocks have doubled in value, some have tripled, and one has grown by a factor of 33. This snapshot of the Mutual portfolio is just a point in time, since prices change every business day and the fortunes of some of these companies are changing as you read. This portfolio took more than fifty years to build and is worth more than $2.5 million (or $400 per "unit"). And not a single Wall Street professional, mutual fund manager, banker, or financial planner crafted this fluid masterpiece of stock investing.

Although it appears to have the patina of luck in finding a few good companies, Mutual is not atypical in its triumph. More than 60 percent of investment clubs regularly beat the performance of the Standard & Poor's 500 index (S&P 500), which is the benchmark to beat for most professional large-fund managers. What's even more remarkable is the fact that only 20 percent of professional stock mutual fund managers have beaten the S&P 500 over the past decade. What do investment clubs know that the pros don't? Their "secrets" are rather simple:

1. By investing small amounts in stocks on a regular basis, your cost of entry—through dollar-cost averaging—gives you an edge over those who jump in and out of the market.
2. Selection of high-quality (well-managed) companies whose earnings and dividends are growing consistently is the best long-term investment.
3. By holding on to profitable stocks and reinvesting dividends and gains, you're compounding your investment for the future.

The basic NAIC credo comprises these tenets. It all translates into the language of wealth when repeated often enough over decades. This formula works because the long-term trend of the stock market ever since stocks have been traded is a perpetual *upward* (though jagged) curve. Bonds won't beat it; they usually don't even outpace inflation. And you can forget about money market funds, bank savings accounts, certificates of deposit, and U.S. Treasury bills. Stocks are the train that will take you where you need to be when you need the money the most.

"Start as early as you can, even if you're retired, because you may have twenty years ahead of you," O'Hara asserts. "Don't worry about saving only small amounts. Don't get discouraged."

The growth-stock movement has helped people from all walks of life who have little to invest. Although started largely as educational forums, investment clubs have given hundreds of thousands of investors the tools they need to provide for a comfortable retirement and a multitude of material needs.

A Protestant minister approached O'Hara at an investment fair in Chicago a few years ago to thank him.

"I asked him why he was thanking me," O'Hara recalls, his eyes dancing like a leprechaun's. "He was living in a $500,000 home and had bought a new car for $20,000 out of investment savings of $220,000. By using investment club teachings, he was able to build his portfolio over thirty years on a salary of $3,000 a year."

---

Investfact: Americans aged forty-five to fifty-four average only $2,300 in financial assets. U.S. Federal Reserve Board chairman Alan Greenspan called the national savings rate "the key domestic economic policy problem of this country."

---

# CHAPTER 7

# What a Good Stock Looks Like

The Chicago NAIC council is turning people away because they can't seat any more than 650 for lunch. A nearly standing-room-only crowd faces Barry Murphy, the NAIC's marketing director, as he takes the podium and begins showcasing companies vying for investors.

"The average investment club member holds a stock 7.3 years," Murphy barks confidently in his Boston accent. "But the average institution holds a stock for lunch."

The assembly chortles with approval. This is a diverse lot of casually dressed adults ranging in age from twenty to eighty and representing every ethnic stripe. Since they're looking for good companies to invest in, they like hearing about companies that are looking for long-term investors.

After a few words of encouragement for the converted and not-yet-converted investors, Murphy introduces the first speaker: James Karman, president of RPM, Inc.

This Ohio-based company is a rising star among investment clubbers. Hardly a household name, it produces coatings, waterproofing, and craft materials for a staggering variety of applications. Its most visible products are probably its Testor plastic models, Bondo auto-repair products, and Day-Glo paints. It also recently purchased Rust-Oleum paints. What it lacks in widespread recognition, it makes up for in blissful balance sheets. And with a string of forty-seven years of growth in sales and earnings, it's easy to see why RPM is one of the largest NAIC club holdings.

Karman is gesticulating with take-charge hand movements as he recites the canon of RPM's financial prowess. He and his executives have cultivated club investments through talks at two thousand investor club fairs like this one. He knows that once these shareholders buy the stock, they'll hold on and buy more through RPM's DRP. Two decades of doing these fairs has produced a loyal following: some twelve thousand club members buy the stock through NAIC's low-cost purchase plan.

"Twenty years ago, you could get 100 RPM shares for $1,000," Karman says. "Today that same investment has grown to 2,250 shares worth $45,000, which includes $1,200 in dividends."

The group is reverent in its silence as Karman recites the rest of RPM's (1993) numbers:

- earnings/share up 14 percent
- sales up 16 percent
- compounded earnings growth 17 percent
- company's compounded rate of return of 25 percent has beat S&P 500 for every year since 1977
- about 20 percent of total sales come from foreign markets in seventy-five countries
- twenty consecutive dividend increases
- four thousand employees in the stock ownership plan

Karman continues to flout the company's dominance in each of its market segments. The pie charts on his slides are steaming with profits. His speech concludes with his declaration that RPM's board of directors consists mostly of outside directors, has $200 million in working capital, and never borrows to finance operations. It has even eliminated $100 million worth of businesses that didn't fit into its strategic plan. Following a short video highlighting RPM's success, he opens up the lecture to questions from the audience. A handful of queries probe whether the company sells "ozone-safe coatings," why it stays on the NASDAQ, and if it's focusing on overseas growth. The audience may be impressed with the company's track record, but they're also thinking of future growth.

Next up is a relative newcomer in the NAIC universe. The assembled investors tune in to another rosy pitch, wondering if *this* company is the one that will spark their portfolio.

## FUNDAMENTAL ANALYSIS

Most investment clubs follow the principles of fundamental analysis, a system that evaluates earnings and price movements. Based on these principles, let's look at some of the ideal characteristics of a perfect company:

1. The stock can be bought at a fair or discounted price, relative to the market and the competition.
2. There's double-digit potential for (market) price appreciation alone.
3. The profitable company is one that continues to post growth

of at least 15 percent per year in earnings and earnings per share.

4. Management is so astute that they are increasing market share by introducing new, profitable products into the market on a consistent basis. This inspired management team is diversifying and enhancing shareholder equity while expanding sales and profit margins. In fundamental analysis, growth is a prime consideration in nearly every aspect of a company's business.

5. The company is "recession proof" because it sells products and services unaffected by business cycles and bought by consumers no matter what the economic climate.

6. The company is exploiting growth in overseas markets and sells its products in established and developing countries with minimum adverse impact from currency fluctuations.

7. The company has shown its passion for small investors by paying fat dividends (for decades) and consistently raising that dividend.

8. The company provides shareholders with a no-cost, direct-purchase dividend reinvestment program.

9. The company's annual report is forthcoming, with every relevant detail on operations laid out in a concise and straight-forward manner.

10. The company sells a quality line of products and services that will be in constant demand and current with the latest technologies. The company also is a model corporate citizen that nurtures communities and countries in which it operates through generous donations and by not polluting or depleting natural resources beyond a sustainable level.

Does any company meet all of these criteria? No. But it's a good place to start before you "run the numbers" in analyzing price and earnings. This information is found in annual and 10-K reports. That should be your first stop before you do the more involved analyses on price, dividends, and earnings (see page 131).

---

Investfact: Only 52 percent of "baby boomers" and 37 percent of "baby busters" have developed a financial plan, according to a national survey by the Equitable Assurance Society.

---

## HOW TAFFY EVALUATES COMPANIES

No two members of Betty Taylor's family investment club live in the same state. They include four generations from Washington State to Georgia. They correspond through the mail.

Betty Taylor and the seventeen members of her family are perfect examples of successful investment clubbers. Everyone from her ninety-four-year-old father in Lincoln, Nebraska, to her three children (and their spouses) and nine grandchildren are involved. The club, based in Overland Park, Kansas, a suburb of Kansas City, is named "Taffy"—for "Taylor Family Investing." Starting in 1987, the club has had an annual average return of 28.9 percent, compared with 11.26 percent for the S&P 500 stock index.

Taffy started in the "Black Monday" year, but that didn't bother Betty, an investor since 1960. "We were quite new to investment clubs when the market went down, but we weren't concerned. You know that you don't sell if you have good stocks."

Betty, a retired teacher, has started a club in nearly every place she's lived along the way from being transferred from one midwestern city to the next with her husband, Robert, who's now retired from the Burlington Northern Railroad. Now she's an avid teacher of stock investing across the country.

"I now teach eight- to twelve-year-olds investing. You'd be amazed at what they learn. It's very rewarding."

One winner in the Taffy portfolio turned out to be Home Depot, which was bought at a $4 average base cost. The club picked up the idea from Betty's son-in-law in Georgia (where Home Depot is based), who noticed that "the stores are always busy and provide good service." They've also scored with Wal-Mart, McDonald's, GE, and 3M. The club has won several performance contests sponsored by the NAIC.

Like most experienced NAIC members, Taffy abides by the rules of their *Stock Selection Guide*, which Betty insists "saves a lot of errors." Additionally she has her own checklist when evaluating a company:

- Plot sales, earnings, and profit margins and pay special attention to pre-tax profit.
- Look at the industry a company is in. Is it going to be around a while? Does the company have a niche within the industry?
- Look for debt to be relatively low—under 33 percent of capital.
- Earnings growth should be at least 15 percent to 20 percent.
- The "current" ratio should be two to one or greater. That means that company has two times more assets than liabilities.
- Avoid "penny" stocks and companies that have less than five years of operating figures.
- Don't sell good stocks (even if they slide for a while). Let the

profit grow. But sell the dogs. This is the hardest thing for clubs to do.

• The good companies that don't pay dividends are okay, too, as long as they're putting money back into the company to make it grow.

If stock analysis is a bit of a fog bank at first, keep in mind the rewards if you stick to it, Betty advises.

"It's never too late to get started. If you do your homework, you can do better [than a professional]. There's no other place than the stock market to get such a good return."

## FINDING GOOD COMPANIES TO EVALUATE

It's not hard to find promising stocks. Some interesting companies are mentioned in your favorite business newspapers and magazines. You can't wait to get going. Now the fun starts.

Start finding out where your prospective stocks are headquartered and request their annual reports and 10-Ks through their investor relations departments. Your best resource at this stage is the *National Directory of Addresses and Telephone Numbers*, which is published by Omnigraphics in Detroit. Your public library should have this book in its reference section. Other key resources are the Standard & Poor's directories (under many titles). Larger libraries may even have annual reports on file, so it helps to befriend your reference librarian.

*Value Line* and *Barron's* are important secondary resources, also available in your library.

## WIC

The Women's Investing Club (WIC) of Cincinnati, begun in 1980, features a number of mother-daughter teams that fine-tune their research skills through stock-picking contests within the club. Six teams of three enter the annual event, often producing exciting results. Member Nona Reed scored the highest in the last contest, picking Elcor Corporation, which makes roofing materials. She made her pick one month after Hurricane Andrew hit south Florida. Her gain was 242 percent. Two other picks did nearly as well.

One often mentioned outlet for members who can't sell—or buy—within the club is to make a purchase on your own. Mary Jane A'Hearn, president of WIC, bought Telefone de Mexico (Telmex) at $.83 a share after it privatized. It has gone on to become one of the biggest gainers for investors in the last half decade before it slumped in 1994–95. In this case, her own diversification in an international issue proved to be a profitable choice.

## READING ANNUAL REPORTS

The good news about annual reports is that they're free and packed with useful information. The bad news is that they tend to be self-congratulatory and hide useful information. What's an investor to do? Read between the lines. This is a skill that takes some practice, but it can be learned with experience.

If you want to skip most of the corporate hubris, read the 10-K report first, a black-and-white version of the annual that is more concerned with numbers than glossy photos of executives and products (see following section). This is what the company must file with the Securities and Exchange Commission (SEC), so the flowery prose is edited out.

The first thing to keep in mind is that the annual report is as much a piece of marketing literature as it is a public record. You'll find nearly everything you need to know about earnings/share, earnings, dividends and various liabilities, and ratios. It can be quite daunting, though, especially when you get to the back of the report. Let's start our tour of these reports with the major sections:

## Financial Highlights

This is a snapshot of the company's financials. The specifics on each category are in the back section under "Financial Review, Statements, and Notes to Consolidated Statements." So the highlights are a summary of all the back matter. It's generally a positive sign to see increases in sales and earnings per share. In the report, this is what you'll typically find:

1. *Net sales.* This is total revenues minus expenses due to operations. This figure contrasts with "gross" sales, which is not as meaningful. As with most of the numbers in this section, you'll get the past two years side by side.
2. *Earnings before taxes, or pre-tax income.* This is the company's profit before it pays Uncle Sam.
3. *Net earnings.* This is the real profit figure, or post-tax earnings. This is what the company gets to keep after all taxes and other expenses are subtracted from gross revenues.

4. *Net earnings per share*. This is the profit divided by the number of shares outstanding. This accounting principle is designed to show you how profit translates into individual shares. Like all the other numbers, if this figure shows a year-to-year increase, that's good.

5. *Research and development expenditures*. This is how much a company spends on developing new products and services. It's also expressed as a percentage of sales, which is more meaningful.

6. *Fixed-asset expenditures*. This is what the company spends on things like new plants and equipment.

7. *Working capital and current ratio*. This is money not tied up in debt that's available to the company for running its operations. The ratio expresses a percentage of that capital on a per-share basis. This is an important figure that shows the liquidity of the company.

8. *Return on average invested capital*. This number seeks to express how a company performs relative to the money invested in it. Double-digit figures in this department are considered excellent, although it varies for every industry. Average invested capital is defined as stockholders' equity plus long- and short-term debt minus short-term investments (cash). In a nutshell, this figure attempts to show if investors are getting a good return on their stakes.

9. *Percentage of net debt to net debt plus equity*. Also known as the "debt-to-equity ratio," this number indicates the relationship of debt to equity ownership. A high ratio shows a high degree of leverage (borrowed money). That means when a company's sales and profits drop—especially in a recession—the bankers will be pounding on the door. This puts

more pressure on management to perform and take higher
risks.

10. *Book value per share.* This probably won't be of much interest
to you unless you're a value investor (the subject for several
other volumes) and hunting for a bargain. This valuation gives
a per-share approximation of what the company would be
worth if every chair, pencil, and plant had to be sold tomorrow. There's a lot of tricky accounting involved in arriving at
this value, so it doesn't help you that much.

Keep in mind that every company states its financials slightly
differently, although each one must state fundamental things like
sales, net sales, net earnings, earnings per share, working capital,
and other relevant measures. For more detail on every one of the
these categories, turn to the back section of the report, which is
nothing but numbers.

## Management Discussion

This is the spot where you'll see some swell pictures of the top
two or three executives—usually the chairman, chief executive,
and chief operating officers. This is management's opportunity to
tell shareholders what a wonderful job they did over the past year
and how they will continue their good deeds in the future.

Reading between the lines in this up-front section, scan for
management changes, management's view of earnings and sales,
and any other highlights. You'll need to get beyond corporatese
like "our employees represent our most valuable asset . . ." and
"we best serve our stockholders . . ." If the company has taken a
hit because of sales declines, product failure, or other factors, it
may be alluded to in this section. To get the real meat, however,

you'll need to jump to "Review of Operations" and the financial statements. Companies usually place the serious talk about money in "Management's Discussion of Results" in the back of the report.

The front section should describe each sales segment in detail (unless the company sells only one product or service). It should also be broken down by division, geographic region, or product line. This section should show how much progress the company is making in selling its wares. The better annual reports give quite a bit of background on the products and market demand and something about the competition (don't expect too much here). The more technical the product, the more plain English you need.

The more succinct reports will skip a lot of the background, however. For this kind of detail you'll have to search the 10-K, where the company must explain what it does and sells. Some basic questions for this section include

1. Are the company's lines of business faring well? Has the company introduced new products for new markets?
2. What is the market for new and existing products? Is it expanding or shrinking? Has the company expanded into new (overseas) markets?
3. How do the company's sales break down by market segment? Look for a bar or pie graph. Is the company focused heavily on one segment? What are the growth rates for these segments? Is the company engaged in any joint ventures, licensing arrangements, or franchising? How will these enterprises impact revenues?

## Review of Operations

This boils down the front section to the essentials. It explains what sold when, where, and how in a few short pages. Information should be broken down by segment, listing sales, orders, and pending business. Again, this terse body of information gives you a few clues as to where the company's going.

1. Compare sales per sector or segment to the importance of the segment within a company. Say, for example, a company's largest segment is cellular phones and it's losing sales to the competition (fewer orders than last year). That could spell an earnings hit in the future if the company doesn't make up the slack elsewhere.

2. Look for new segments. These are the new businesses. How much is the company spending on them? When do they expect to break even? How much will they lose? You'll probably have to refer to the financial statements to unearth the real numbers on these operations. Smart companies make these new enterprises a small part of their overall business. They're wise not to bet the farm. Some of these new segments, however, may represent the future of the company.

3. Check for expansion of facilities or employment. This is a great sign that things are going well. Conversely, layoffs or plant shutdowns may indicate trouble in a particular market or segment. Corporations don't expand and build new plants unless there's a proven and expanding market for their products. This could be a huge factor in reading the company's future. If you break down facilities changes by segment, you can get a picture of what direction the company's taking. A

powerhouse electronics company like Motorola, for example, is building new plants all over the world, which is a result of robust growth. In contrast, defense manufacturers in the United States are closing plants and laying off people. This section is also called "strategic investments."

## Results of Operations, Liquidity of Capital Resources

Now we're into the back room of the report, where all the most important business is discussed in the dryest possible terms. This is what to look for:

1. *Profits.* This fundamental word has many faces. Operating profits describe money gained by what the company does. Many companies make money on other investments, but this is the number that says what they earned from their principal activities. Another useful measure is "net margin on sales," which should show a year-to-year increase. It's rare for this to be in double digits. If it is, the company is doing quite well. Profit margins are also important yet are difficult to decipher unless you know what the averages are in particular industries. They vary quite a bit. For example, pharmaceutical margins are traditionally quite high; fast-food margins are pretty tight.
2. *Sales.* Again, there are many ways of examining this number. Sales per employee, for example, is a measure of productivity. Expanding companies should show gains in this area, which shows that they're not spending too much money maintaining and growing a skilled workforce.
3. *Working capital, liquidity, capital resources, and net cash provided by operations.* This is the money that pays the bills and fuels some expansion. A company rich in cash also has a

cushion to weather recessions, currency fluctuations, political problems, huge lawsuits, and other unforeseen liabilities.
How much working capital and cash is enough? You'll get a
fierce argument from corporate accountants on this one. But
it doesn't hurt to see the corporate kitty rising relative to
sales. A company producing record amounts of cash is doing
well. These days a company can sell more stock and bonds
to raise money, so this should be noted carefully. "Debt-to-
equity ratio," on the other hand, should be declining—especially long-term debt. This number is the total shareholder's
equity divided by total liabilities. Most companies try to stay
below a one-to-one ratio. The "current ratio," in contrast, is
a similar comparison that shows how much cash can be
coughed up to pay liabilities. Good ratios should be two to
one or higher. The more cash a company has, the more flexibility it has in responding to dour markets and introducing
new products (that may fail).

4. *Research and development, capital expenditures.* It's still true
that you have to spend money to make money. This one's simple. If sales and profits are rising dramatically, so should R&D
and capital expenditures (new assets, equipment, and plants).

5. *Independent auditor's report.* Every financial statement must
be reviewed by an independent auditor, but for some reason
most every one of these statements finds nothing wrong.
Skip this little exercise in bureaucracy unless it's headlined
"We found a crook!"

6. *Consolidated earnings and stockholder's equity.* By now we're
in table format. These give better breakdowns of expenses,
depreciation (tax write-offs), and interest. The net earnings
are still the most crucial numbers. Stockholder's equity indicates outstanding value of shares and dividends paid.

7. *Consolidated balance sheets/financial statements.* This table is an elegantly simple statement of the company's business. There are two halves: assets and liabilities, or how much they own and how much they owe. Some noteworthy line items include accounts receivable (money owed for products/services sold), assets, and inventories. Year-to-year increases in every item is positive. Liabilities cover everything from debt to stockholder's equity. Cash flow gives you an idea of where the money's going and how much is left at the end of the year. Any number in parentheses represents a negative number, which isn't necessarily bad unless earnings or "net cash" is negative.

8. *Notes to financial statements.* Here's more detail on all of the aforementioned financials. If you're a good detective, this can be the most interesting part of the report, since bodies are often buried in these footnotes. Getting past the explanation of the accounting methods, debt/credit instruments, foreign currency gains/losses, and tax breakdowns, you'll find some nuggets like "contingent liabilities," for example. These gremlins could be anything from big lawsuits to other shenanigans not discussed anywhere else in the report. One footnote led a *Wall Street Journal* reporter to an executive who was actively embezzling from the company. You'll find juicy items like executive compensation (or how executives become multimillionaires no matter how poorly the company performs), environmental liabilities (toxic dumps they'll have to pay to clean up), product liability suits, and shareholders suits. Most of these particulars will be dismissed with "this item will not materially impact the corporation," but keep an eye on them anyway. Some suits have resulted in CEO sackings, company restructurings (Sears) and Chapter 11 filings (just about any company that sold asbestos). No

company is proud of their footnotes, so pay special attention to them.

## SECRETS OF THE 10-K

This document may be as dry as sandpaper, but it's frank and concise. It's also the best place to flesh out some of the company's liabilities. For example, most annual reports will devote only one sentence to "contingent liabilities" such as lawsuits and super-fund toxic waste sites. Inside 10-Ks, however, you'll find a much more detailed examination of these problems and how the company thinks they will impact their bottom line.

Most individual shareholders don't bother to ask for a 10-K or 10-Q (the quarterly version). But under federal law, companies must disclose any activity that will materially impact—cost it money—its operations. Again, when you ask for an annual, also ask for the 10-K. Shareholder relations departments are required to provide it but won't automatically send it along with the annual. Ask for it by name. This report details company information that may just be footnotes in the annual. It's especially useful in pinpointing pending or ongoing litigation or regulatory problems. A lot of this information is not found in annual reports.

## OTHER KEY DOCUMENTS TO WATCH

### Notice of Annual Meeting and Proxy Statement

Companies send out these documents to shareholders, and you can't get one unless you qualify: you must be a shareholder of record prior to an annual meeting. At least one share gets you in the door. Most of the notices and proxies are routine business, and companies seem to make them as dull as possible. However, it's a good idea to vote your proxy or attend an annual meeting if you can. It's an invaluable experience in the whole process of corporate governance.

Proxies—or rights to vote a certain number of shares—usually ask you to approve management's slate of a board of directors, auditors, stockholder proposals, and incentive plans for executives and employees. You can vote against every proposal whether management supports it or not. This is the closest thing a corporation gets to democracy, although the vast majority of management proposals pass easily. Proxy votes are usually cut-and-dried affairs if a company is doing well. But if the company's showing a steady decline, vote for change. Discuss this with your club members. You should decide on how to vote your proxies.

Your proxy represents votes based on the number of shares you own. So the more you own, the bigger your vote. And no matter how many shares you have invested in a company, you have the right to propose your own slate of candidates to the board and even vote for yourself. Several "dissident" stockholders have done this in recent years. A notable example is Sears Roebuck, which was forced to restructure after a dissident shareholder rattled the top floor in Sears Tower. He started lining up opposition by contacting disgruntled institutional investors.

Sometimes, though, dissidents want to take over the whole company. While this is the subject for another book, you should view these matters with caution. Takeover artists in recent years have taken over companies, loaded them up with debt, sold off profitable divisions to pay off the debt, and made off like bandits.

Read your proxies carefully. Are new board candidates suggested?
Is a company restructuring proposed?

Some other cautionary areas involve executive compensation.
As a practical matter, you want to reward top-performing corporate executives through stock option plans. It makes them happi-
er because they are much wealthier, and it increases their stake
in the company. It also makes them poorer if they don't perform
well. The bigger the stake those running have, the more likely it
is they'll be more productive and boost sales and earnings.
Employee stock ownership plans are also a good idea. It seems to
have done wonders for previously moribund companies like
Ford. Moreover, profit-sharing plans result in a fat bonus check
at the end of the year for workers and executives who meet certain financial goals. That's good for you, too, as a stockholder. If
they make money, so do you.

A proxy item may also contain anti-takeover measures. If a
company is well managed, this isn't such a bad idea. One popular proxy proposal in recent years has been to add more outside
directors to the board. These are successful executives who are
not affiliated with the company so they're not beholden to anybody on the board or within the company for a lucrative job.
They also provide useful and more critical insights into a company's operations. Unless they are "straw men" for takeover artists
bent on making a quick hundred million, they should be added
to the board to give it a fresh perspective. Most boards don't like
this idea. But it's a sign of progressive management if they welcome outside directors.

## USING RATING SERVICES AND PUBLICATIONS

The more sources of information you obtain on a subject, the better. Granted, the amount of information out there on companies is overwhelming. From SEC documents to *Money* magazine, you can argue that there's probably too much information. One good thing about investment clubs is that there are plenty of people to manage and analyze the information. Annual reports, 10-K's, and other sources can be parceled out for review by group members at the president's request.

So I'm going to focus just on what I consider to be the key sources of public company information. If you lust for more information, feel free to peruse the resources section at the back of this book.

### BARRON'S (800-277-4136/800-544-0422)

Available in nearly every library and at most newsstands, *Barron's* is the savvy older sister of *The Wall Street Journal.* Both are published by Dow Jones, Inc. For most investors, *Barron's* is the ultimate resource for incisive commentary and market minutiae. Every stock listed on world stock exchanges is tracked in the weekly tabloid. You can also find market indexes, insider transactions, and mutual fund news. You can chart economic and business trends against stock prices or look up the highest-yielding money market fund. All of the "tabular" information (quotes, prices, indexes, and the like) are in the center section of the magazine. In the "wrap-around" section are features, commentaries, and news items.

The features and columns range from investigative to downright witty. This magazine should be a staple of your research efforts. Here are some tips on navigation:

- Read the wrap-around (front and back) sections after you scan the table of contents and "index to companies" to see if any company you're following is mentioned.
- For weekly quotations, check the "Market Week" section. You'll find all listed companies on every exchange plus mutual funds, U.S. Treasuries, bonds, money market funds, top savings vehicle yields, indexes, and economic data.
- Of particular interest to investment clubbers is the "Market Laboratory" section, which lists P/E's and yields for all indexes; earnings estimates and earnings "surprises"; stock price charts; and commentary on every market.
- The publication offers a free annual/quarterly report service on selected stocks. For information, call 800-965-2929/800-965-5679 fax).
- Features cover trends in markets and industries. Their periodic surveys of money managers ("Roundtables") are especially rich sources for stock ideas.

## THE WALL STREET JOURNAL (800-221-1940)

For most investors, The Wall Street Journal is the alpha and omega of business information. Not only is it a rich source of news on companies, earnings, and market trends, but it gives a generous amount of tips and guidance as well. More user-friendly than ever, the Journal should be used in concert with local business sections, magazines, Barron's, and Value Line.

Although you can obtain stock quotes from any business section, the depth of reporting in the Journal is unrivaled by most national news organizations, with the possible exception of *The New York Times*. The *Journal* has its reporters in boardrooms, on trading floors, and in the dark alleys where the most valuable rumors are whispered. Pick it up in the library or have your club subscribe to it.

## THE "A" SECTION

This front section is reserved for news and editorials. The front page has two columns of news briefs, one trend story, one "lightweight" story (usually in the third column from the right), and an in-depth story that could feature anything from junk bond mischief to hospital administrative abuses. Breaking news is always inside the "A" section. The back of the section is reserved for political coverage and staunchly conservative editorials.

## THE MARKETPLACE/"B" SECTION

This middle section contains subsections on advertising, health, law, management, the workplace, personal investing, demographics, the environment, technology, design, and consumer purchasing patterns. This is the best place to track business trends. You can find everything from company profiles to short, snappy columns on humorous subjects. Check the back of the section for interesting tidbits on companies. Check the "Index of Businesses" on the second page of the section to see if your stocks are mentioned in news stories.

## MONEY AND INVESTING/"C" SECTION

This is the heart of the paper, where all of the financial and commodity market results are posted. "Abreast of the Market" offers an overview of what happened in the previous day's trading, highlighting trends and big moves. There's also complete coverage of credit markets, mutual funds, commodities, small stocks, and options. If it's traded on an exchange anywhere in the world, this section will list it. Look for "Corporate Dividend News," small news items, discount brokerage ads, mutual fund quotations, "Dow Jones U.S. Industry Groups," the "Dow Jones World Stock Index," and "Heard on the Street." If you want to be sure of getting a high price on a stock, buy those mentioned in the "Heard on the Street" column. You and a million other investors will be getting a really inflated price. If you want a quick scan of the markets, read this section's "Markets Diary." This gives you a concise look at one-day to one-year market trends around the world. It's the handiest feature of the *Journal*.

- If tracking companies, check the company index to see if and where it's cited in the paper.
- Check current market prices in the "Market" section.
- Earnings reports are always buried in the front of the "Market" section.
- Quarterly roundups highlight the most active winners and losers.
- If a company merits a front-page story, it's often a market mover.
- Never buy a company after a positive mention in the paper. About two million other readers will have the same idea and push up the price.

## THE *VALUE LINE INVESTMENT SURVEY*
(800-833-0046)

Also available in most libraries, *Value Line* is a subscription periodical whose forte is fundamental analysis (earnings, growth potential, and so on) of stock data. Once you've picked companies to study, *Value Line* becomes a close friend and associate.

Unlike *Barron's* and *The Wall Street Journal*, *Value Line* is a rating service that publishes its data. Commentaries and 1,700 company reports are delivered in weekly sections. The reports on specific companies are accompanied by separate "Selection and Opinion" reports, which focus more on market trends and larger groups of stocks. They'll tell you if a company is poised for growth and estimate how much.

The heart of the Value Line service is the company reports, which combine a graphic display of earnings trends with an analysis of the company's prospects. These reports allow you to compare a single company against industry data and historical trends. *Value Line* identifies companies that are solid performers.

Along with basic fundamental data like earnings per sale and sales figures, Value Line provides ratings on financial strength, safety, timeliness, price stability, and earnings predictability. The three main parts of the *Value Line Investment Survey* are a summary and index; selection and opinion (of specific companies); and ratings and reports.

Using the service for the first time can be a little daunting, but it's invaluable once you get the hang of it. Here are some guidelines:

• *To find a company, you can search the index either by company name or industry.* Value Line groups companies into industry groups, from advertising to water utilities. The industry groupings are important to see how individual companies rate among their peers in terms of P/E's, yields, earnings, and sales growth.

• *Pick a company according to timeliness, growth, yield, and safety.* Within these criteria, *Value Line* applies several "screens" to further categorize stocks. The service provides lists and analyses of timely, conservative, high-yielding, cash-generating, best-performing, low/high P/E, high total return/dividends, high return on capital, growth, and "bargain basement" stocks.

• *Check the key ratios and estimates.* These include current P/E, estimated yield (next twelve months), estimated earnings, estimated price range, and beta (market risk).

• *Read the industry reports, then the company reports. Value Line* provides a timely overview of what's happening in a particular industry. Then you can relate it to a single company to see how it compares with its peers.

• *Other relevant information* includes earnings per share, revenues, dividends declared, splits, cash flow per share, capital spending per share, market share, net profit margin, debt, and total return projections.

• *Don't Use Value Line as a decision maker.* Sometimes they miss a few things. Run your own numbers. The service provides several estimates and targets, but use your own judgment. And remember that hundreds of thousands of other investors are using the same service, so it could make certain companies "popular"—and not necessarily good buys.

• *Probable relative price, yield, and appreciations are good yardsticks. Value Line* will project a three-to-five year "target price." Use it as a guideline only. You also need to evaluate management, an area in which *Value Line* is weak.


## READING STOCK QUOTES

To locate a stock quote, first find out which exchange lists the stock (NYSE, AMEX, NASDAQ, and so on) and use the company name or symbol to locate it in the alphabetical listings. Keep in mind that some small stocks are listed under "NASDAQ Small-Cap Issues" or the "pink sheets," which are not in every paper. Most companies will tell you on which exchange they are listed. For our purposes, you should probably stay away from pink sheet stocks. It's difficult to find quality analysis on them.

**52-Week**

| High | Low | Stock Symbol | Div. | Yield | P/E | Sales | High | Low | Close | Change |
|------|-----|--------------|------|-------|-----|-------|------|-----|-------|--------|
| 15 | 10 | BUN | .20 | 2(%) | 5 | 600 | 14 | 13 | 13¼ | +1 |

The first category gives you a yearly price range in dollars per share.

The stock and stock symbol are usually different. Stock symbols are used by brokers to locate a stock in the computer.

The dividend is the annual per share amount paid.

Yield is the dividend divided by the closing price.

P/E ratio is the price divided by earnings per share. If there's no P/E, the company's losing money.

Sales measured trading volume in hundreds of shares.

High is the highest price the stock traded at during market hours; low is the opposite.

Close is the price the stock was quoted at when the market closed for the day.

Change shows the difference between the opening and closing prices.

(Note: How to evaluate these numbers is explained in the following section.)

## EVALUATING MANAGEMENT

Management is the brains, heart, lungs, and liver of a corporation. Without it, even the best product in the world won't get sold. Quality management also keeps the company profitable and innovation alive and thriving. In this way, along with earnings and market price, management is the "third key" of selecting a promising stock.

Earnings and steady price appreciation are a subset of superior management. Without the guiding intelligence of management there is no consistent earnings growth and the stock will probably languish. So when you're buying a company, you're buying management first and foremost.

"Buy a logical theory of management," Tom O'Hara advises, "because if the company grows, sales and earnings grow."

Management is such a multifaceted enterprise that it's difficult to measure. A company may have astounding earnings for one year and fall off the map the next. This is a particular problem with technology-oriented companies. If management doesn't keep up, it gets buried in the marketplace. Quality management can see into the future, know what it does well, and keep all its soldiers marching in the same direction.

If a management team can master the operation of a modern corporation, it is playing the instrument to which a corporation will sing the dulcet song of capitalism. It may well be easier to define a consummate concert violinist than excellent management. Nevertheless, here are some criteria:

### Advertising

This is the part of marketing that presents a company's case to the world in fifteen seconds or less. With millions of messages bombarding business and consumers every year, that short burst of information must sell a product or service. It's got a lot of competition. Good advertising can make the difference between obscurity and dramatic gains in market share. Credit Wendy's International's "Where's the Beef" commercials for putting that hamburger chain on the map in a country bursting with hamburger chains. To be good in this business is to be unforgettable. The best ads creep into your subconscious and stay there up until the point of purchase. That may sound sinister, but it makes the cash register ring. Some ways of evaluating advertising include

- **Does the company produce effective advertising? Do the ads translate into sales? The annual report may give you a clue; outside analysts usually provide more insight. In other words, has advertising boosted business? By how much?**
- **Do the ads "sell" the product or service? That is, do they make you feel good enough about yourself or the product/service to want to buy it consistently? This is also one of the easiest aspects of a company's management to evaluate, although it's mostly a subjective process.**

## Adaptation to Change and Quality Standards

Though a tough nut to crack, this is essential in measuring how a company will perform in the future. To dissect this management variable, you need to know something about a company's business. Analysts' reports and newsletters cover all sorts of specialized industries and can help you evaluate business even if you don't have a background in the subject. Without a doubt, a company that doesn't adapt to change is begging bankruptcy. Some good questions to ask are the following:

- How is management keeping up with changes in markets, technologies, and global economies? What management changes have been effected to adapt to change?
- Does the company employ "total quality management" techniques in instituting the continuous process of improving its operations?

Some of the top international manufacturers are qualifying for standards under the "ISO 9000" program, which will enable them to sell more effectively in the European Common Market. Look for this notation in annual reports. One of the best examples is Motorola, which two decades ago was thought of as a staid manufacturer of radios for military and government. Throughout the last twenty years, though, it adapted to changes in the marketplace by making the highest-quality microprocessors, hand-held telephones, and communications networks in the world. As a result, a $100 investment in Motorola in 1988 grew into nearly $500 by the end of 1993, easily beating the S&P 500 and its competition in the electronics industry.

## The Chief Executive Officer

Who is the top dog, and how is he/she doing? This person not only is in charge of running the company, he/she is usually chairman of the board of directors. In public corporations this means that person runs the company and answers to stockholders. It's not difficult to find information on top CEOs. Business magazines profile at least one of them in every issue and at least once a year in special sections. This person should have some success in working with people and organizations. If they have brittle egos, that could lead to trouble. As captains of the ship, they can't afford any mutinies. The best CEOs often take credit—and deservedly so—for productive teams that they assemble. Some legendary CEOs in this mold include Ross Perot (when he was with EDS), Jack Welch (GE), Bill Gates (Microsoft), and Thomas Watson Jr. (IBM). In evaluating a CEO, judge by what their team has done, not by all of the hubris in annual reports. Remember, even top-notch CEOs don't last forever.

- **Has the CEO accomplished what he or she set out to do over the past few years? Read the back sections of annual reports and 10-K's for the truth of the CEO's performance. Does the individual in question have some ability to motivate or transform the company so that its performance has improved dramatically or remained consistently good?**

## Marketing and Sales

If a company can't sell what it makes or services, it's not going to survive. Marketing involves researching products, the market for those products, and selling them effectively to customers (ideally for repeat business). Sales is what happens when marketing does its job. Other than measuring sales volume, you can examine marketing efforts by looking at how a product's being sold. Typically, the more "channels" a company has, the more opportunities it has to sell its product or service. For example, a company like Wendy's International sells through either company-owned or franchised outlets. You won't find Wendy's hamburgers in a Sears store. Microsoft, on the other hand, sells through software dealers, mass merchandisers, catalogs, and computer superstores. It's difficult to walk into any retail outlet that sells computers and *not* see a Microsoft product. Some key questions to rate the company's marketing efforts include the following:

- Is the company finding more markets for its products (overseas, new applications, and the like)?
- Have their efforts resulted in increased sales? Are their products generating more sales/employee through increasing direct sales, licensing, franchising, joint ventures, distribution, or royalty arrangements?
- Is the company increasing or losing market shares for all of its product/service segments? How is it faring against the competition?

## Research and Development

No company can keep making the same product the same way year after year and hope to stay solvent. Markets change. Technology changes. Buyers become more sophisticated. If a company doesn't spend money to develop new products, it'll become less competitive. Some companies have to remake and "reengineer" themselves before they can make new products and offer services. GM, Chrysler, and Ford needed the success of Japanese cars and the alienation of their traditional customer base before they retooled their unreliable product lines in the 1970s and 1980s. GM even started a new division from scratch—Saturn— in order to entice customers from Japanese compacts. Other companies seem to cultivate a genius in developing perfectly ordinary yet remarkably useful products. Rubbermaid, a housewares pioneer, claims to bring to market a new product for every day of the year. Minnesota Mining and Manufacturing (3M) has introduced everything from sandpaper to cellophane tape, mostly unglamorous things that most companies would have over-looked. AT&T's Bell Labs invented the transistor, which led to the computer chip. A corporate culture that leads the way in product innovation not only consistently boosts profits, it creates new markets for products that have never existed before. You should know these things about a company's product development:

- Are its new product lines successful in garnering market share? Innovation is worthwhile only if these products sell. Apple introduced its first Newton notepad computer in 1993, but it was shunned by the market.
- Does the company have a "culture of innovation"? How is that reflected in new product introductions? Does the company have promising new products in development? For drug companies, for example, this is known as having products "in the pipeline." A company like Abbott Labs has a number of new drugs and medical diagnostic instruments that allow it to enhance its market position.
- What is the company spending on R&D? This number is in the annual report and is best expressed as a percentage of sales. For manufacturers in technology or health care products, a double-digit percentage is considered excellent; 7 percent to 9 percent is good.

## Strategic Planning

What is the company's long-range "mission"? Where does it want to be in the next five, ten, and twenty years? Is it streamlining to concentrate on core businesses? Kerr-McGee, for example, sold off its uranium mining business to focus on oil, gas, and coal exploration. Most companies say that their mission is to "provide attractive return to stockholders," but what does that mean? Here are some critical questions:

- **Is the company buying new businesses or selling existing ones in keeping with an overall strategic plan? Does it plan to dominate certain markets? How does it plan to do it? Is it downsizing or streamlining to fatten revenues and reduce operations costs? What are the costs of these moves in terms of write-downs or loss carry-forwards (see accounting notes in annual reports)? How is the company increasing productivity of employees and increasing overall efficiency (see environmental concerns below)?**

## Environmental and Social Responsibility

Nearly every company pollutes in some way in the normal course of operations. Our industrial society was set up to waste more than it produces. But companies that are actively managing environmental problems are also saving money and increasing profits. Two of the best examples are 3M and Dow Chemical. Their annual reports are loaded with details on how much money they've saved through pollution prevention programs. Part and parcel with a company's environmental responsibility is its social responsibility. That translates into charitable and community development activities. Philip Morris, Mobil, and Texaco are huge sponsors of the arts. In this regard they are also conducting some marketing. The more attention a corporation pays to the communities it serves, the more customers it will attract to support it. On the other hand, nearly every large company pollutes on a large scale. If this area is a great concern to you, weigh the tradeoffs carefully. You'll also need to know the following:

- What are the company's liabilities for pollution under the Superfund Act? This is a difficult question since the law is constantly changing. The back section of the annual report should note if it's a "party to litigation." You need to know how much this litigation will "materially impact" earnings. Remember the companies in the asbestos business? Massive litigation forced them into bankruptcy.
- What is the company doing to improve energy efficiency and reduce waste in every aspect of its operation (such as recycling, for example)? Again, this is a bottom-line concept since most corporations use and waste tremendous amounts of energy and natural resources.
- Has the company signed on to the CERES Principles (environmental responsibility and audits)? Has management conducted environmental and energy audits and taken steps (spent money) to improve problem areas?

## Customer Service

This is really a form of marketing. It takes much less money to hold on to current customers than to bring in new ones. You have to keep your customers happy and coming back for more, no matter what business you're in. This is where "total quality marketing" and "benchmarking" come in. A top company establishes standards for excellence and constantly rates employees and the methods they use. Some companies live and die by customer service. Home Depot is an excellent example. When you walk into one of their home center stores and have to find something among tens of thousands of items, you need help. That's why Home Depot trains its people well. Wal-Mart has employed a similar concept. Unlike most discount mass merchandisers, which let you roam around the store unfettered, Wal-Mart features smiling "sales associates" who greet you at the door and in the aisles to give you a shopping cart or help you find something. There are hundreds of good examples of customer service in our service-oriented culture, but you'll be hard-pressed to find them in annual reports or other documents. You'll need to see customer service firsthand. Other considerations include:

- **Does the company produce a high ratio of repeat business?**
- **Does the company have a problem with defects, returns, or recalls in its manufactured products? Does it quickly take these products off the market or wait for a government-forced recall? One sure sign to look for is the Malcolm Baldrige award for quality (past winners have included Motorola, Eastman Chemical, and Cadillac).**
- **What's the company's system for monitoring customer service?**

---

Investfact: The majority of all NAIC chapter clubs beat the S&P 500 and most stock mutual funds in the 1980s. Nearly 70 percent beat the S&P 500 in 1992.

---

## HOW THE INTRINSIC
## VALUE CLUB RATES MANAGEMENT

With three young daughters, Stephen Beer is concerned about future weddings as well as college tuition. So he's doing all he can to invest for the future as a member of three investment clubs in the New York metropolitan area. He's also investing in three separate accounts for his girls.

The New York NAIC council, which he founded, has around four thousand members. Compare that with the Milwaukee area, which has more than ten thousand members, but only one-tenth of the population of New York. A glance at the NAIC's "All-Star" list reveals a preponderance of clubs in Ohio, Michigan, Illinois, California, and Texas. Very rarely do clubs on the East Coast appear on the list, though. Stephen thinks people may have a different attitude about investing on the East Coast that may not lend itself to the club culture.

"I'm not an expert on the culture of the Midwest, but it seems they like to get together for the social aspects. Here in the Northeast, everyone wants a quick profit. I beat myself for years trying to understand why we couldn't draw more people to investor fairs. They [people in the area] feel that they know it all already or else they're afraid to learn."

Despite what he perceives as the prevailing attitude toward investing, Stephen has worked hard to build the NAIC's base in an area dominated by the financial industry. Most of the major banks and brokerage houses have their headquarters in downtown Manhattan. He's a taxi ride away from companies whose sole purpose is to sell financial products—and not necessarily knowledge. Nevertheless, he's been successful in building up the NAIC's presence in New York, New Jersey, and Long Island. He started stock investing right out of college in 1981. He is a member of three clubs, two of them "model" clubs open to the public and designed to show investment club techniques to all comers.

Stephen's work has paid off so far; he's been given the honorific title of "president emeritus" of the New York Council and has appeared on CNBC, CNN, and Fox television to promote investment clubbing. The thirty-six-year-old is also working on recruiting younger members into the fold.

As a certified public accountant, he can read balance sheets better than most. It has helped that he started out his career as an assistant portfolio manager with a Manhattan-based mutual fund. Ironically, the fund's manager introduced him to investment clubs, bringing him into the "Intrinsic Value" club, which consisted of New York police detectives who had been investing since 1971. He estimates the club's annual average return to be 12 percent.

Being an accountant, he's particular when it comes to a balance sheet. To him a financial statement is like a Where's Waldo? game, where it's hard to find the most elusive information. But he can zero in on a problem quickly. This acuity helps him identify management strengths and weakness in a matter of minutes. Here's what he examines:

• *Where is the growth coming from?* He looks for "the pipeline where earnings and sales growth is headed." That ultimately focuses on new products, services, and markets.

• *Cycles are important as buying opportunities.* In other words, he pays attention to business and economic cycles only if they make an industry "out of favor." He cites the pharmaceutical industry as a good case in point (at time of publication). It's been bombed by the market from 1992 to 1994. Only in 1995 did it begin to move up again.

• *Use the NAIC's* Stock Selection Guide *as a "springboard."* This tool is designed merely to give an idea of how a growth company shapes up. Don't forget to check if the company's price is in the "buy" range.

• *Use computers whenever you can.* Not only will you save time, many packages (such as the NAIC's SSG-Plus) include the stock data with the program. Stephen has found that new members who do the SSG by hand "quickly lose initiative." Although he likes the NAIC's analytical packages, he recommends Quicken as a better package for record keeping. It's widely available at computer and discount stores with computer departments.

• *Cash flow is one of the most important indicators of a company's health and growth potential.* To an accountant, cash flow measures a company's financial strength but isn't used as much as it should be to gauge a company's management, Stephen notes. "A company can always push up earnings through creative accounting, but can't bring [through accounting methods] more cash. A healthy cash flow is good for dividends, earnings, and stock buy-backs."

• *Look for changes in the "current" ratio.* This relationship of assets to liabilities should be in a positive range. Keep an eye on it to see if there are any significant changes.

• *The amount of debt may not be critical.* "I would want good management before I looked at debt."

• *Be realistic in your expectations for growth in the future.* Stephen aims for companies with sales growth of 10 percent or better, with earnings growth always exceeding that. More important, management should be dedicated to growth. Good examples of growth-oriented managements include Home Depot and McDonald's.

• *Look for companies with relatively lower P/E's.* These numbers could land you some bargains.

Although his own portfolio is down somewhat the last two years thanks to his having picked a series of battered consumer stocks, Stephen is confident that he'll see a rebound, a message he's eager to pass along to new investors.

"When I see people who previously had no investment knowledge come to a club meeting and defend a stock, that's the one aspect of investing I enjoy the most. Although clubs are not an area in which to concentrate most of your wealth, they're good for discipline and as a base for education."

## STRONG MANAGEMENT IS WHY McDONALD'S IS SUCH A GOOD INVESTMENT

Occasionally there's a moment when a stock maintains great fundamentals and keeps on doing it year after year no matter what the rest of the world is doing. This kind of company is the classic "bottom up" kind of pick. Its performance continues through every business and economic cycles's attempts to sink it. Such a stock is McDonald's, which has nested in the NAIC's Top 100 list for several years and led the list in 1994. It was also the company most often named by individual NAIC members as their most profitable investment.

Anybody with common sense, though, can see that there are plenty of places selling hamburgers and fries. You can get this meal anywhere from the corner coffee shop to yuppie nouvelle restaurants. The hamburger is as ubiquitous as billboards on expressways. Moreover, in light of the unhealthy fat content of its most popular products, what keeps McDonald's going? More to the point, in the face of intense competition and changing demographics and dietary patterns, how does the company keep making money?

McDonald's has perpetuated a certain culture that keeps growing, especially overseas. It's not just that people love their main fare; it's that they can expect the same thing from a McDonald's whether it's in Oak Brook, Illinois (their corporate world headquarters), or in Beijing, China. They also won't have to wait long or pay a lot. But just what is so good about making billions of hamburgers, fries, and shakes?

When I had a chance to visit McDonald's "Hamburger University" in Oak Brook, I obtained some insights into how the great burger machine operates. In a nutshell, the company relies on what any good investor needs to succeed: consistent discipline. For McDonald's, discipline translates into standards that *every one* of the more than fourteen thousand restaurants must follow. There's a long list of them: everything from the proper temperature for deep-frying potatoes to measuring the exact volume of a soft drink is standardized, monitored, and constantly updated. It all starts in "Hamburger University."

Embraced by ponds and trees, the "U" offers a prairie-style hotel, non–McDonald's restaurants, and recreational facilities. The locals even come to fish in the adjacent lake. There's a McDonald's art gallery in the conference center, featuring expressionist renditions of fast-food themes. There are even quiet places to unwind after a long hot day training over a grill. This is where it all begins. All the managers and franchisees must graduate from this institute of culinary learning.

The results of this program are startling. McDonald's has created in the fast-food industry what Microsoft has accomplished in software and what Motorola has done in cellular phones: an instantly recognizable product that does nothing but build market share and sales. Oh, and the earnings aren't bad, either. Here's the menu of Mac's sizzling numbers:

- As the largest food service organization on earth, the company has reported 30 years (119 consecutive quarters) of record systemwide sales and profit per common share.
- Over the past decade, shareholders have enjoyed a 19.8 percent compound annual return.
- Systemwide sales were $25.9 billion in 1994, accounting for 7 percent of all U.S. restaurant sales and 2 percent of all U.S. restaurants.
- The company split the stock two for one on June 24, 1994, and boosted the dividend by 12 percent. It was the eleventh split since the company went public in 1965.
- Operating in more than seventy countries, they are rapidly expanding their overseas market share. There are McDonald's restaurants in Iceland, Israel, Saudi Arabia, and Slovenia.
- Their compound annual growth rate for overseas earnings hit 23 percent in 1993 on sales growth of 19 percent. The company is adding from 900 to 1,200 new restaurants *every year*.

To most investors, these numbers suggest a long-term buy and hold unless there are management or market changes. But even though the picture looks good now, it doesn't hurt to look ahead.

The "Stock Barons" (whom I visited in Des Plaines, Illinois), for example, posed some valid questions about the company. Ironically, the Stock Barons were meeting only a few blocks from one of the original McDonald's. The Barons' queries are in line with what any investor should ask even their best performers:

- McDonald's is weak in the evening meal business segment. What are they doing to improve their position? Will their experimental launching of stand-alone evening restaurants do well or fail?

**Investfact: Companies Most Often Named by Individuals as Their Most Profitable Investment (Source: *Better Investing*)**

1. McDonald's
2. AT&T
3. General Electric
4. AFLAC
5. Wal-Mart
6. Wendy's International
7. Exxon
8. Disney
9. Procter & Gamble
10. Dominion Resources
11. PepsiCo
12. Philip Morris
13. Coca-Cola
14. RPM
15. Abbott Labs
16. Merck
17. Motorola
18. Allied Group
19. Blockbuster Entertainment
20. GTE
21. Kellogg
22. Chrysler
23. Paramount
24. Telefonos de Mexico (Telmex)
25. Southwestern Bell

- The company has had mixed to poor results in introducing new products. Some notable failures have been pizza and Chinese food. What are they doing to improve their product mix?
- The company is not well diversified in other businesses. It's basically a restaurant chain. What would be "strategic fits" for the company that may insulate it from any downturns in their main business? Does it make sense for them to be in the entertainment business?

## HOW TO KNOW IF THE PRICE IS RIGHT

Other than making the initial review of a company's management, you'll want to buy it at a good price and try to predict where that price will go in the next five years and beyond. At this stage in the game you've already determined

1. if sales are growing at a consistent rate;
2. if earnings are growing;
3. if earnings per share are growing.

It's time to pull out your crystal ball, which to most stock pickers is their calculator. Club investors will want to find stocks that show certain characteristics:

- *Ideally, your stock's price will double (100 percent growth) every five years.* That translates to a growth rate of at least 14.4 percent a year. It's easier if you round that off to 15 percent a year. Value Line and other services will readily provide this data.
- *Eventually your portfolio should be diversified among large, small, and internationally active (deriving more than 20 percent of*

*sales from overseas markets) companies.* Put about 25 percent of your investments in each type of company and use the remaining quarter for a mixture of speculative stocks.

• *Ideally, the large-company stocks should pay dividends, which you can reinvest to buy new shares.* Combined with annual growth rates of 7 percent to 12 percent, the dividend income should help you achieve your annual goal of 14.4 percent or more.

In terms of numbers, look for the following:

## Growth Rate

A traditional growth signal is *sales growth*. Earnings and stock price usually climb steadily if sales are on an upward track. Although double-digit growth rates are the most desirable, 5 percent to 7 percent is acceptable for large companies. Younger or technology-driven companies, however, often record annual sales gains of 20 percent. The question is, can these rates be maintained? Competent management can keep this curve pointing skyward for years.

## Pre-Tax Profit

This is profit before the government taxes sales. You'll also need to compare your companies' pre-tax margins with those of similar companies in the same industry. Sometimes a pre-tax margin that lags behind the industry average is good, especially if you think management will be able to turn that situation around. Again, consistency is important. If a company is unusually profitable or has taken a hit on margins, is it going to change soon?

The annual report, 10-K, and outside analysis are useful resources on this question.

## Profit on Invested Capital

You want this ratio to be as high as possible. Companies that post 10 percent to 25 percent returns on capital (the sum of all classes of stock) are making productive use of your investment. Again, you'll need to compare the company's return on capital to its competition. Is it making the grade? If it isn't, what is management doing to raise this ratio?

# HOW TO ANALYZE PRICE

The number crunching you'll need to do on price analysis is complicated until you get used to it. You'll need to do it to ensure that you're getting a fair price for the stocks you're considering.

## Earnings Per Share

This ratio is one of the foundations of fundamental analysis. Ideally, earnings/share should be growing the same rate as sales. While it's often beneficial to find companies with low earnings/share relative to its industry group—this could signal a bargain—that measure is often debated. High-growth companies typically have double-digit earnings/share, so they may be a bargain (in terms of stock price) in the early stages of their development. If you're going to track earnings/share, try to project its five-year path. *It's a good idea to buy a company when a company's earnings are beating analysts' expectations.*

## Dividends

The dividend (also see pages 159–170, on dividend reinvestment plans) serves two purposes. It represents a portion of earnings—up to 50 percent—that are paid back to shareholders. More established companies use fat dividends to hold on to shareholders and as a safety hedge in down markets. Bear markets tend to pummel the prices of low-dividend stocks first. A company that pays dividends from 4 percent to 6 percent is also likely to grow in the future. Look for companies with consistent dividend growth.

## Price Range

When you read the stock listings in the newspaper, you'll notice "highs," "lows," and "closes" after the stock symbol (among other numbers). These numbers represent the stock's price range. The "52-week" highs and lows show the range over one year. Using the worksheets on the following pages, plot out the highs and lows over the last five years.

When you invest in a stock, you're rolling the dice. You're usually betting that the price will go up. If you chart sales, earnings/share, pretax profit, and price history, you get a picture of what that stock's likely to do. You can either use the NAIC's charting tools (see resources section) or rely upon the Value Line service. In any case, you need a visual representation of the past, present, and future. Your bet is placed based on your confidence in the company's management, as reflected by "the numbers." That's why it pays to analyze financials and the price range.

All other things being equal, provided there's a consistent level of management in a quality company, you can reasonably assume that the stock price will continue its upward trend. Of course, you can always get derailed by rising interest rates, economic downturns, and business cycles. These market factors most dramatically impact "cyclical" stocks, which depend upon business and economic cycles for a lion's share of their growth (see section on cycles, page 185). For example, if the economy is unhealthy, nobody's going to be rushing out to buy cars, clothes, boats, appliances, or any number of consumer "durables." Chemicals, financials, paper, and steel are other industries affected by business cycles.

The two best ways to avoid getting burned on price are by *not* buying *only* because the price is rising, and by *not* selling because the price slides. Obviously a great many would-be investors ignore this advice. These are the most common reasons nearly half of clubs fail.

### Break-Even Possibility

What are the odds of breaking even on the stock you're eyeing? How many years has the stock sold at or above its present price (adjusting for splits)? If it's at least three out of five years, you have a good chance of breaking even.

### Upside/Downside Ratio

This number gives you an idea of how low and high the stock price might go given its history. It also assumes that it will catch at least one uptrend in the business cycle over the next five years. Consider this factor in concert with the other tests listed here. The following worksheet can be used to plot the characteristics of a company's financials and management. Use it for each stock to compare and contrast each company. If you want to save time, use some of the computer programs suggested in the resources section at the back of the book. The basic data should be available through Value Line or Standard & Poor's.

---

# WORKSHEET
(copy and use per each stock)

**COMPANY:**

**Sales Growth**                    **Average (5-yr.)**

_____                       _____

*Note: Double-digit growth is desirable.*

**Pre-Tax Profit on Sales**         **Avg.**

_____                       _____

(net income before taxes divided by sales)

**Profit on Invested Capital**      **Avg.**

_____                       _____

(earnings/share divided by book value)

**Price History**                   **Avg.**

_____                       _____

(range/highs and lows)

---

## ANALYZING P/E RATIOS

For investment clubbers, the price/earnings (P/E) ratio is a useful tool in measuring a company's investment status and potential. Like most financial statistics, the P/E ratio is not an island unto itself. It is meant to give you a relative picture of where a company stands within an industry or the market as a whole. How "high" or "low" P/E's are depends upon the earnings of the company and P/E's of similar companies.

## WORKSHEET QUESTIONS:

For each stock evaluated, is the trend up (+), down (–), or flat? Compare a company's five-year historical figures.

|             | +   | –   | Flat |
|-------------|-----|-----|------|
| Sales Trend | ___ | ___ | ___  |
| Earn./Share | ___ | ___ | ___  |
| Price       | ___ | ___ | ___  |
| Avg. Trend  | ___ | ___ | ___  |

NOTE: *You should have at least* five years' *worth of price earnings history per company. This should include high/low prices, earnings per share, price/earnings ratio, dividend per share (with percent payout and yield), and the average and current P/E ratio. Check Value Line or Standard & Poor's for this information. This is a preliminary judgment of management based on sales/profit trends (up, down, or flat), profit on invested capital, and price trend. Based on this information, should you explore or abandon this stock?*

[  ] EXPLORE          [  ] ABANDON

To calculate a P/E, divide the stock price by earnings per share. This information is available from the company or from the financial sections of newspapers. Therefore, a $10 stock with earnings of $1 per share would have a P/E of ten.

As a rule of thumb, the companies with P/E's that are lower relative to their peers may be better buys and poised for growth. This is not a hard-and-fast rule, however. Some smaller, high-growth companies have relatively high P/E's, but that doesn't mean they are bad investments—unless they stop growing. You have to look at P/E's within the context of management strength, sales growth, earnings growth, and the market/economy at large.

P/E's are a fairly dependable point of departure for other analyses but they are highly cyclical; they move up and down with business and economic cycles and are not sole indicators of a company's health. For example, P/E's mushroom during periods of high inflation and when the economy is coming out of a recession. Some companies themselves are cyclical by nature (see page 185) and may sport low P/E's because they are at the bottom of a business cycle. The P/E is only one part of the whole. Where is the company going overall? How is it growing? Is the growth consistent? Is management consistent? Weigh all these factors.

William O'Neil, author of *How to Make Money in Stocks*, found that the best-performing stocks didn't necessarily have the best P/E's. More than 95 percent of his winners had a higher-than-average P/E and either a new product or management prior to a price gain. He pays more attention to earnings growth (25 to 50 percent per quarter) and solid companies with high brand recognition. Conversely, Gene Walden, publisher of the *Best 100 Stocks Update* newsletter, found that a group of low P/E stocks provided an average total return of 8.4 percent versus -1.6 percent for a high P/E group.

P/E's quoted in newspapers represent "trailing" earnings (past history); stock analysts refer to future or projected earnings. Typically, stocks expected to post above average growth will carry P/E's that are similarly above average. Interest rates also impact P/E's (see chart page 140). Generally, in low-rate environments P/E's tend to be higher, and vice versa. That's because stocks compete with interest-bearing vehicles in the marketplace. Investors are willing to pay more for earnings when interest rates—and inflation—are low or falling because of the potential for a better return over fixed-income investments. So a high or low P/E by itself should not be the deciding factor on whether to buy or sell.

# CHAPTER 8

# How Smart Money Picks Stocks

Mary Barrett Beck's "Smart Money" club in Fort Lauderdale won the NAIC's "All-Star" competition three years in a row. Having served two terms as president and volunteered hundreds of hours of her time to the more than fourteen thousand members of the Southeast Florida Council, she has a good grasp of what makes a club prosper. She requires a commitment on the part of every member to learn the ground rules of investing. The retired English teacher should know. She's tripled her money in less than ten years.

"We insist that prospective members go to council programs. We want to make sure they're NAIC investors and not traders. Then [when they join a club], we tell them that they must make a twelve-month commitment or they won't get their money back. We're not interested in a person who drops in and out."

You may recall what investment clubbers call the "Rule of Five." Of five stocks being eyed for future value, one may be unacceptable, three may perform as expected, and one may exceed expectations. This is a bedrock principle in diversification. You can't control what a stock will do or what markets will

**137**

do to it. But you can spread your risk among several picks using the same method of picking them. Mary says that she follows this opening guideline closely. And those who watch stocks carefully are bound to find one that shows "explosive growth."

She also tells members that they must become "specialists in one or two stocks." That means they not only follow the financials and news reports, they must call the company after any big move in price. Companies often have an explanation. At each meeting they make their recommendation to buy, hold, or sell. When they're not monitoring stocks, they're learning about new facets of investing. Six months of their monthly programs are devoted to education, the other half to examining new stocks. Occasionally they even get out to have some fun while in the process of being educated. That means field trips.

Since Blockbuster Entertainment's headquarters (since bought by Viacom, Inc.) is nearby, the Smart Money members stopped in on their annual meeting, emceed by the dynamic CEO Wayne Huzienga. Mary describes the meeting in 1960s parlance: "It was a 'happening.'

"There were three screens displaying a multimedia presentation in the Ft. Lauderdale Performing Arts Center. Then they gave out a compact disc of famous songs and the *Aladdin* video sequel. Then they started talking up the amusement park Wayne is building. We hope Blockbuster will be like Disney. When it started to expand, we doubled our money."

The club also visited a lesser-known but local company called Sensormatic, which makes corporate security systems. They've even talked to the company's officers, who now welcome investment club shareholders because they are less volatile investors than institutions. Individuals rarely sell at the end of a quarter to provide "window dressing for the portfolio." Mary says it gives her members even better information about the stock when they can see the company and its management.

Her investing acumen extends down into three generations of her family. She has given stock to her six children and thirteen grandchildren. She's even in the process of uniting her far-flung family through a club communicating with electronic mail on CompuServe. They'll send information and vote on club matters through the computer network in what is sure to become the investing mode of the twenty-first century.

She came to stock investing reluctantly, though. Her father, an intelligent engineer, "lost his shirt in the 1929 crash because he bought on margin [with borrowed money]. For a long time, I figured if *he* couldn't make money in the market, then I couldn't." But she changed her tune later in life when she adopted stock investing as a hobby.

Mary emphasizes that picking stocks is something anybody can do at any point in life. She's worked with the young and the old. Sometimes she discusses Disney's stock price with her twelve-year-old granddaughter, Tandy. And recently she helped a seventy-three-year-old woman set up her computer for stock screening. She notes that "the women of my generation let their husbands do the investing, but we [women] can do a better job. We're more detail oriented. And we do the work."

> **Investfact: One of the most popular gifts among investment clubbers for their children, grandchildren, or godchildren is buying stock in their name. It will give them an important lesson in saving, especially if the stock offers a dividend reinvestment plan.**

# Annual Interest Rates and P/E Ratios

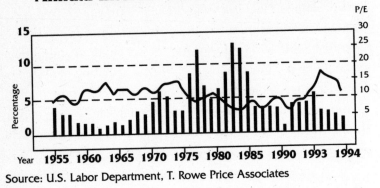

Source: U.S. Labor Department, T. Rowe Price Associates

## BALANCING RISK AND REWARD

In order to determine if a stock is worth holding over the long term, you need to balance a few factors. Stock market prices gyrate in cycles, depending on market conditions, business cycles, and interest rates. So buying a stock at any point in time is a dicey proposition unless you can balance risk and reward— and buy the stock at a good price. Remember, the name of the game is buy low and accumulate wealth.

A five-year estimate of where a stock may be headed is based on the assumption of at least one business upcycle and recession every five years. This section will help you use the information you've already compiled to project the best price range in which to buy the stock in question.

Use the numbers you've compiled for the previous worksheet to arrive at estimates. Especially important are the highest and lowest P/E's and price ranges over the past five years. While this process is not 100 percent accurate, it will offer you some idea of what to expect from a company given its past performance.

## Determining the Best Price Range

**A. Estimate the High Price** (over the next five years)
   Avg. high P/E____ x est. high earnings/share =
   *Forecast high price* $ ____

**B. Figure Low Price**
   Avg. low P/E____ x est. low earnings/share = ____
   Avg. low price of last five years = ____
   Recent severe market low price = ____
   Price dividend will support present dividend divided by high yield
Note: *Divide the present yield by the highest yield over the last five years.*

   *Forecast low price* $ ____

**C. Zoning: How to Select a Good Price** (use figures from above)
   ____ High forecast price minus
   ____ Low forecast price =
   ____ Price range
   1/3 of range = ____

   **BUY** RANGE: Lower 1/3 = ____ to ____
   **HOLD** RANGE: Middle 1/3 = ____ to ____
   **SELL** RANGE: Upper 1/3 = ____ to ____
   Present market price ____ is in the ____ range.

**D. Upside/Downside Ratio** (potential gain vs. loss)
    High price ____ - present price ____ = ____ divided by
    Present price ____ - low price ____ = ____ to 1.
      *U/D ratio* = ____ *to 1.*
Note: A U/D ratio of less than three to one is unfavorable.

**E. Price Target** (where the price can go)
    High price = ____ divided by
    Present price = ____
    ( ____ - 1.00) x 100 = ____ (% gain)

## Dividend Safety Test

This test will show what you can expect from the dividend. Typically, the more income, the greater the safety—and total return.

**A. Full Year's Dividend $** ____ **divided by**
    **Current stock price $** ____ **=**
    ___ **x 100 =** ___ *present yield or % returned on purchase price*

**B. Average Yield over Next Five Years**
    **Avg. earnings/share next five years** ____ **multiplied by**
    **Avg. % payout** ____ **divided by**
    **Present price** ____ **=** ____ **%**

**C. Total Return**
    **Five-year appreciation potential** ____ **divided by**
    **5 =** ____ **%**
    **Avg. yield** ____ **%**
    **Total return** ____ **% (five years)**

*Note: Although a hefty total return is desirable, not all companies will have a good dividend. Newer companies, in particular, are not known for paying generous dividends. This is but one factor of many to weigh.*

## Summary Checklist

The following list will help you complete your decision-making process. In addition to the worksheet information, weigh these factors evenly:

1. Is the company new ____ or well established ____?
2. The company operates domestically ____ or internationally ____?
3. The product/service line is broad ____ or narrow ____?
4. The company sells to consumers ____ , business ____ , or government ?
5. The company is a dominant ____ or minor ____ player in its industries?
6. The company and its products have high ____ or low ____ visibility to the public?
7. The stock is listed on the NYSE ____, AMEX ____, NASDAQ ____, or regional exchanges?
8. Price records are available going back five years ____?
9. The company's dividend has been continuously paid dating from ____ (year)?
10. The company's businesses are established ____ or new ____?
11. The company's potential is based on new products ____, international expansion ____, or demographic trends ____?
12. Sales and profits fluctuate widely ____ or within a narrow range ____?

13. Capital invested per dollar of sales is high ____ or low ____?
14. Price competition within company's industry is intense ____,
    moderate ____, or minor ____?


## The Final Analysis

*The bottom line:* Do your tests indicate
[  ]  a potential return of 100 percent gain in five years (at least
      20 percent/year)?
[  ]  consistent earnings, price, and price/earnings growth?
[  ]  a favorable upside/downside ratio?
[  ]  a favorable current price?
[  ]  a favorable dividend and dividend growth rate?


*What course of action should we take?* Overall, based on evaluating all these questions, this company has excellent ____, moderate ____, or poor ____ investment potential.

If you're making this presentation to your club, this is the ultimate question to put to a vote. The system isn't foolproof, but it's
derived from more than forty years of use by the NAIC in its
*Stock Selection Guide.*

## DIVERSIFICATION

If you think that you can ensure the safety of your portfolio by loading up on defensive stocks, you're probably making a mistake. A better way of lowering your risk in a buy-and-hold approach involves diversifying. Diversification is as simple as not putting all of your valuables in one vault. The same holds true with stock investing. Don't concentrate your holdings in one company, industry, region, or country. The rules of diversification are straightforward. Here's how they work:

- *Not all of your holdings should be concentrated in one company.* This may be most difficult for new clubs, but it's the most important rule.
- *Don't concentrate more than 20 percent of your holdings in any one industry.* In larger portfolios (ten stocks or more), aim for 10 percent industry concentration.
- *Obtain some international exposure to partially insulate yourself from market downturns (see section on international investing, page 152).* Several U.S.-based companies earn a high percentage (20 percent to 80 percent) of their income overseas. Some examples include AFLAC, McDonald's, Motorola, and Procter & Gamble.
- *Don't place all your bets on "blue chips" (established large industrial concerns like P&G and Philip Morris).* Companies with sales under $1 billion—called "secondary" issues—stage rallies independently from larger companies (see following section). About one-third to 20 percent of your portfolio should contain these issues. Although most clubs focus on blue chips, secondary issues should not be ignored.

## The Power of Small Caps

When it comes to General Motors or General Electric, there are few secrets. Every time an executive sneezes, it makes headlines. That's often a negative factor. Often Fortune 500 companies like these don't have the latitude to innovate or restructure the way they should because of corporate culture, ingrained attitudes, and fear of institutional sell-offs if they spring "earnings surprises" on the market.

In contrast, small-capitalization (generally stocks with market capitalizations under $1 billion) stocks offer growth potential without the circus of attention that follows their every move. For example, when Microsoft was first listed on NASDAQ, it was a small cap. Because they're typically not followed by large brokerage houses or analysts and are listed in lower-profile markets such as the American Stock Exchange or the NASDAQ electronic market, their prices are largely unaffected by NYSE-league traders who dump multimillion-share "blocks" in a single transaction.

Small caps are often much less volatile than their S&P 500 cousins. They also outperform the big boys as a group. Over the last sixty-five years, small caps averaged about 12 percent annually, compared with the Standard & Poor's 500 index average of 10 percent, according to Ibbotson Associates. Moreover, small caps have outperformed large stocks in every period following a recession since 1954. If you're achieving the (minimum) expected return of 12 percent per year, your money triples in nine years seven months.

That means a $50,000 portfolio would become $150,000 in under ten years. Long-term investors reap the largest rewards from small caps. The "small firm effect" is a phenomenon that has been proven by researchers who note that over the last sixty years, stocks of small-capitalization companies have been the leading category of *all* stock funds.

Small stocks represent few household names. You won't find a single IBM or Sears among them. Usually, the best way to find these companies is through mutual funds. The resources to fully examine these stocks aren't widely available to the individual or club investor.

A small group of fund managers specialize in picking small stocks, which typically have under $500 million in market capitalization. According to Morningstar's tally, there are only 156 small-stock funds in the 4,400-fund universe. Most of them aren't fawned over like the $30 billion–plus Fidelity Magellan fund, which Peter Lynch managed to greatness by buying small caps. Yet over the past three years (through 1994) this group of funds has posted a 12.36 percent annual return. Only technology sector funds (20.38 percent) and financial funds (16.81 percent) have done better in this time period. You can, of course, build your own small-stock portfolio—or include small stocks as a portion of your holdings—but it takes more research and patience.

The basic premise of small-stock investing is simple. As the economy grows, so do these companies, which are responsible for 75 percent of new jobs in the United States. Relative to blue chips, small stock prices grow proportionately larger because they are often priced lower relative to the big boys.

In a time of low inflation, large companies simply can't grow that much. Moreover, the giants are downsizing to pare their costs because of shrinking markets. Small caps often have lower operating costs and higher profit margins. That translates into double- or triple-digit earnings growth.

If you want to boost your small-fund portfolio, consider funds that employ the "value" approach to stock picking. These bargain-hunting managers buy strong companies that are underpriced relative to the market. Consequently their picks often outrun similar stocks with higher prices during the last stages of a bull market. The Fidelity Low-Priced, Mutual Beacon, and Delaware Value funds are good examples of this approach.

It's difficult to do well in small-stock funds with a horizon of less than ten years. Small stocks typically boom over three- to six-year periods. If you want to diversify properly, you should have at least 20 percent of these stocks in your portfolio if you're under fifty and from 5 percent to 10 percent if you're older. The percentage depends upon how much risk you want to take and how long you have to invest. For your club, it will also depend upon how much time the club wants to devote to small-cap research. It can be more time-consuming.

Small-cap stocks are where most new technology is being developed. They move fast within their own unique cycles. The best funds—and stock pickers— find the newest and latest so that your portfolio isn't napping when the next wave hits. Here are some key facts on why you should add small caps to your portfolio:

• Over the past sixty-seven years, you would've made money in small caps in forty-six of those years, or 68 percent of the time, Ibbotson reports.

• In thirty years, your small-cap portfolio would've beaten any other financial investment. Of course, you have to hold on to capture those gains. Small caps can lose as much as 20 percent (as a group) or gain up to 40 percent in any given year.

• More important, small caps move in long cycles of three to eight years, usually coming out of economic downturns. According to the Center for Research in Security Prices at the University of Chicago, there have been five bullish small-stock cycles since the Great Depression: 1933–37, 1939–46, 1963–68, 1975–83, and the most recent one, which started in 1990. In each of those cycles the small caps beat the S&P 500 by at least 10 percent (up to 16 percent), with annual average returns ranging from 24 percent to 62.5 percent. You'll also note that these cycles skipped only one decade—the 1950s—while overlapping bear markets in blue chips during the thirties, sixties, seventies, and eighties.

• According to Gerald Perritt's book *Small Stocks, Big Profits* (Dearborn Financial, 1993), during the 1976–83 small-cap rally, those stocks turned in a 33.3 percent compound annual return. Perritt found that if you'd invested $10,000 in the S&P 500 from 1940 to 1991, you would've had $330,350 at the end of the period. That same amount invested in small caps totaled $1.96 million, a difference of $1.63 million. Perritt has figured that if you could invest $10,000 a year and earn 12 percent on it, you'll have $1.03 million after only twenty-two years.

• Other than performance, you need small caps to add diversification to your portfolio. They tend to be less interest-rate sensitive and hold their own when blue chips in the Dow indexes get battered. For example, the Russell 2000 and NASDAQ composite indexes were hitting new highs in March 1994 when a spike in interest rates pushed the Dow 30 Industrial Average down more than one hundred points.

• Small stocks behave differently from the GMs and Exxons of the world. They are usually ignored by large institutional investors and brokers, who concentrate on S&P 500 and Dow Jones index stocks. They move quietly and are usually not followed by *The Wall Street Journal* or other financial publications. That translates into less volatility. Newsletters that specialize in small-cap issues are usually more informative than mainstream sources.

• Executives of small-caps tend to own stock in their companies. They are committed owner-managers.

• Price moves are often dramatic because share prices are lower and experience higher-percentage increases (and declines). Double-digit revenue increases often turn into significantly higher stock prices. It's much easier for a $2 stock to double to $4 than a $60 stock to double to a $120 stock.

• Smaller companies often innovate new technologies (software and biotechnology, for example) better than larger ones. The Western Unions and Westinghouses of yesterday are being outdone by smaller, nimbler rivals.

• Brokerage firms are less likely to push a smaller stock over their recommended list (unless they are making a market for the stock). A warning is in order here. Despite crackdowns in recent years, there are still plenty of "penny stock" promoters who tout essentially worthless ventures to rack up commissions. Also, don't buy any stock that's offered during an "initial public offering." Prices are often inflated during this phase and drop dramatically when it concludes.

• There's limited research, but it's available. To research these stocks, ask for the company's 10-K and annual report. To some degree, a few of the major services (S&P, Value Line) follow smaller caps. Your best bet is often newsletters (see resources). Better yet, if you're not up to the research, small-cap mutual funds provide quality stock picking and diversification (see Morningstar Mutual Funds, listed in resources).

What do you do when it comes to technologies and products that most people don't have a clue about? You retreat to fundamental analysis, buy at a good price, and inspect management with a magnifying glass. This applies to small caps that may not have an abundance of published research.

That's how the "Down the Road" club of Delavan, Wisconsin, found their two big winners, which helped them win honors in the Milwaukee Council's annual investment contest. Delavan is a resort community with a large lake, greyhound track, and hotel.

According to President Debbie Wilson, the club's two top winners—Oracle and Biomet—posted gains of 239 percent and 102 percent (as of this writing). Oracle is a database software maker, and Biomet makes surgical implants. As technology stocks, both have had a rocky ride and don't represent typical club holdings. Biomet's wild price range has gone from 3/16¢ to $32 a share. These two picks have helped their portfolio post an average gain of nearly 50 percent.

Debbie, who got her interest in investing from her father, originally "wanted to get rich quick" when she started her own stock investing program in 1985. But joining the fifteen-member "Down the Road" club helped her change her mind-set, which "took about four years." The club consists of members who are accountants, factory workers, and construction contractors.

Debbie likes technology stocks, performing the necessary research and getting them at good prices when the market swings against them. Her personal portfolio favorites are National Semiconductor and Storage Tek. She says she's become disciplined with her computer, which helps her analyze the more complex technology issues. She even teaches classes on computerized investing through the NAIC computer group. This skill leads her to sell and move on when stocks have appreciated. For example, she bought McDonald's at twenty-four, watched it go to fifty-eight, sold it, and searched for a company "with more growth."

**International Investing**

The world is on the move and creating huge opportunities for investors. By including foreign companies (or mutual funds) in your portfolio, you're reducing overall risk. If you invest in markets that don't track the U.S. market, "you're knocking out about 90 percent of the risk" of investing in stocks, according to Roger Ibbotson, president of Ibbotson Associations. The particulars on overseas investing look promising:

• A portfolio with just 30 percent in foreign stocks gave a higher reward for less risk than any other combination over the past decade, research by Morgan Stanley Capital Research found. As of this writing, though, only 5 to 6 percent of assets of those who hold stock funds are invested overseas.

• From Shanghai, China, to Southeast Asia, there are some 1.4 billion people with an annual gross domestic product (GDP) increasing at almost 13 percent a year. Considering that the U.S. real GDP inched up only 2.8 percent in 1993, the scene in Asia is nothing less than spectacular. By the year 2000 these new consumers will represent one-third of the world's economy. Add to that growing economies in East Europe, India, and the Middle East—and trade barriers dropping throughout the world (NAFTA and GATT)—and you have a climate for international growth.

• To put this development in perspective, by the end of this decade there will be one billion Asians living in middle-class households, according to *U.S. News & World Report*. That's equal to the combined population of North America, South America, and Europe. Moreover, high savings rates, inexpensive workforces, and free-market policies will fuel the growth. Most of this growth is occurring in China, Chile, Argentina, Malaysia, Thailand, Venezuela, Israel, Taiwan, Indonesia, and Pakistan. For example, China is gradually converting to a free-market economy of 1.2 billion. They want cars, telephones, refrigerators, and the other trappings of Western culture.

• Money managers at Smith Barney Shearson found that a portfolio containing 70 percent U.S. stocks and 30 percent emerging markets was less volatile than an all-U.S. portfolio. This mix turned in a 19.3 percent annual return from 1985 to November 1993.

• Most financial advisers are suggesting you hold at least one-third of your stock fund holdings in international or "global" mutual funds.

• A portfolio of 11 percent international stocks; large- and small-cap stocks; bonds; and cash posted an annual rate of return of 10.9 percent from 1973 through 1992, according to T. Rowe Price Associates. In dollars, that meant $10,000 in 1973 grew into $80,000 over that period. In contrast, a portfolio with one-third each in U.S. stocks, bonds, and cash transformed $10,000 into only $64,000. The modest amount of diversification added $16,000 to the kitty.

• Diversifying even a small portion of your portfolio overseas can boost returns and lower risk. Morgan Stanley Capital found that a portfolio with just 10 percent foreign stocks and 90 percent U.S. equities raised annual average returns to more than 17 percent, contrasted with 16 percent for an all-U.S. stock mix.

International markets are best accessed through

1. companies that derive significant portions (more than 20 percent of total) of sales through foreign operations.

2. foreign-based companies.
3. international/global open-ended mutual funds.
4. international/single-country closed-end mutual funds.

While items three and four may be the easiest routes, diligent research will yield some excellent individual companies.

Several quality "brand-name" U.S.-based firms do a handsome business overseas. AFLAC, for example, which markets American Family Life insurance, derives most of its profits from selling long-term care and cancer policies in Japan. Former mutual fund star manager Peter Lynch is fond of AFLAC's potential and involvement in the Japanese market (he affectionately called it "JAFLAC" in a magazine article). One well-known company vigorously marketing overseas is Procter & Gamble, which sells its stable of food, cosmetic, and cleaning products under hundreds of foreign brands.

---

**Investfact: A sampling of U.S.-based companies with foreign sales includes**

| Company | % of International Revenues |
| --- | --- |
| AFLAC | 80% |
| Reader's Digest | 57% |
| Procter & Gamble | 50% |
| Bausch & Lomb | 48% |
| Kellogg | 43% |
| Eli Lilly | 41% |
| Philip Morris | 40% |
| Bristol-Myers Squibb | 34% |
| Carter-Wallace | 26% |

The wild card factors in the international game are foreign currency and political risk. Both domestic-based and overseas-based corporations have little control over this additional risk element. Foreign sales are denominated in the currency of the country of origin. Foreign currency values fluctuate every day, depending on a host of often obscure political and economic variables. It's an incredible game of hedge and speculation played by an elite group of traders in major banks and brokerage houses.

The bottom line is that the earnings from foreign operations are always subject to currency risk. If you hold a foreign stock directly through an American depository receipt—the stock of a foreign-based company trading on an American exchange denominated in dollars—your risk is magnified.

"When dealing with foreign companies, you have to be an expert in foreign currencies," warns NAIC president Janke.

Other than employing risky and complex hedging strategies on futures exchanges, your two best routes around this problem are U.S.-based companies with foreign operations that do the hedging for you, or international/global mutual funds. If you choose route one, you can employ all the analytical techniques taught earlier in this book. If you choose a mutual fund, use a service like Morningstar or check ratings in *Business Week* or *Forbes*.

# CHAPTER 9

## How Dividends Drive Long-Term Stocks

Peter Espejo, a director of the OKI Tri-State (Ohio, Kentucky, and Indiana) Council, was teaching an NAIC seminar in a Cincinnati suburb. He is a compact man who likes a long drag on a Marlboro and the challenge of making money when others are selling.

An analyst with Digital Equipment, Peter had a fully funded 401(k) plan at work yet still became involved with the NAIC in 1986. Having studied accounting in his native Philippines and earned his MBA from Babson College in Boston, he is an enthusiastic student and teacher of investing.

About a dozen people ranging from men in their sixties to women in their thirties listen intently as he flips between overhead transparencies and his lecture.

Like his hero John Neff—the legendary former manager of the Vanguard Windsor fund—Peter is a contrarian. He likes to bet against the tide and buy stocks when business cycles are heading south. Walking through some of the fundamentals of NAIC investing, he puts his own spin on the process, smiling all the way.

"I like to buy out of season when others are selling. I buy according to clearly defined objectives with a cool head to find value."

He reviews some of the time-honored strategies, such as reviewing the *Value Line* reports, watching P/E's and projected earnings, and buying cyclicals when the economy is recovering.

"I once bought Citicorp at nine dollars a share [when it was out of favor] and later sold it at twenty-three," he says, beaming. "I'm also loading up on drug stocks [in disfavor at the time] and like utilities in a bear market."

Having lost $7,000 in 1987, he advises the investors "not to get emotionally involved in a stock." He also monitors a stock's dividend yield as an indicator of strength. He's a devotee of Geraldine Weiss's *Investment Quality Trends* newsletter, which recommends stocks based on dividend growth.

A fan of dividend reinvestment plans (DRPs), he likes to buy small stakes in distressed companies and add to them at relatively low cost.

"If you're going to be in the market, get into a DRP and follow the business cycle," he counsels. "If you keep going to brokers, you'll get 'clocked.'"

A dividend, aside from its powerful compounding value, is a symbol and direct statement of the company's health. If companies are cutting dividends, their profits are sagging. If they're raising dividends consistently, all the other items on their balance sheets are improving. A healthy dividend is often a symbol of pride among companies. The most well-established concerns boast of their unbroken strings of dividends and dividend increases. While some of these companies may have fundamental flaws, dividend records are signs of maturity, profitability, management, and progressive growth.

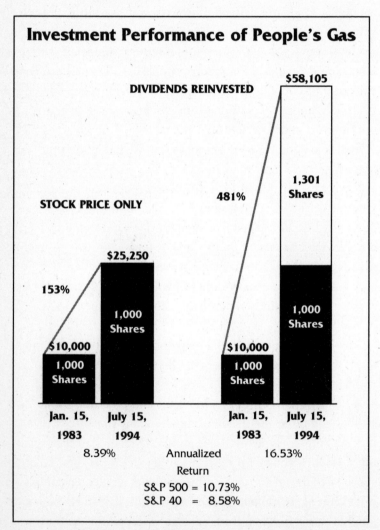

**Investment Performance of People's Gas**

DIVIDENDS REINVESTED

$58,105

STOCK PRICE ONLY

481%

1,301 Shares

$25,250

153%

1,000 Shares

$10,000
1,000 Shares

1,000 Shares

$10,000
1,000 Shares

| Jan. 15, 1983 | July 15, 1994 | | Jan. 15, 1983 | July 15, 1994 |
| 8.39% | | Annualized Return | | 16.53% |

S&P 500 = 10.73%
S&P 40  =  8.58%

Source: People's Gas, Chicago, Illinois

Here's the best part, though. A reinvested dividend compounds your original investment to the point that you're building capital through almost no effort on your part. Let's say you invested $20 a month in different companies and kept reinvesting dividends. After thirty-seven years and $11,280 in monthly payments, you'd be able to spend $35,000 from your portfolio—and still have $71,000 in stock left. If you invest more, you reap more. This is like building a small house that not only increases in value, but builds on additions without requiring costly contractors.

Growing dividends are the icing on the cake because in cases where they too are reinvested, you end up with even more shares. So you're constantly increasing the capital base and your potential for total return (price appreciation plus dividend yield compounded).

A *Better Investing* example of that is the hypothetical purchase of one thousand shares of People's Energy on January 15, 1983, for $10,000. If you make no new purchases, that same block of shares would be worth $31,750 on April 15, 1993, earning you a respectable 218 percent total gain, or 11.93 percent per year. Remember, at 12 percent your money doubles every six years and triples every nine years seven months. If we stopped right here with this example, most investors would be pretty happy with themselves. However, as they say on late-night infomercials: But wait, there's more!

Taking the same purchase over the same period of time—only with reinvested dividends—the final sum is much different. Your initial $10,000 becomes $67,934 over that decade, netting you a 579 percent return, or 20.55 percent per year. Since the S&P 500 index averaged about 12 percent over that period, you beat the market's return by eight percentage points. Most professional managers barely keep up with the market from year to year. Not a bad deal, is it?

The key to this example is consistency. Dividends must be flowing and stock prices must be rising. They don't always do that in the real world. But if you do your research, you'll find the ones that do. Some companies are more consistent in this regard. Some examples of companies that have offered compound annual dividend increases of 20 percent or more (from 1981 to 1991) include Hanson PLC, John Harland, Legg Mason, Philip Morris, Safety-Kleen, UST, Washington Post, and WMX.

## THE POWER BEHIND DIVIDENDS

The increasing value of stocks is powered by a growth engine, and dividends are the turbochargers. They provide the extra kick that makes stock investing that much more powerful. You already know how stocks beat inflation and provide the best returns for financial assets over time. Dividend reinvestment plans (DRPs) provide the torque that keeps turning dividends and contributions into compounding vehicles over time.

As a key principle of club investing, dividend reinvestment is one of those unglamorous mainstays that don't sound like much. But when you examine the relationship of dividends to reinvestment and compounding, it's not hard to see what a beautiful and elegant concept it is.

Dividends are paid by profitable companies to add value to the equity ownership in a company. By making the stock more attractive, dividends stabilize the stock price to some degree so that large institutions and investors alike have a reason to hold the stock for long periods of time. Since stock is a form of capital representing an investment in the company, it's not a bad thing to retain loyal investors to capitalize the company further when it needs to expand (and consequently sell more stock). So the dividend is like using the "carrot and stick" approach to investors. In other words, the company is cutting you a check for a percentage of its earnings. Companies like to attract and keep investors this way. They realize that capital appreciation isn't constant; dividends can keep investors aboard during some of the lean years.

## DRPs: THE SMART INVESTMENT ALTERNATIVE

It's no coincidence that some of the most popular companies among NAIC members offer generous DRP programs. These companies also have worked closely with the NAIC to promote connections with clubs and individuals.

In 1993 the NAIC launched an "Own a Share of America" program that involved 165 companies and NAIC's fifty-eight regional councils. A video public service announcement reached some forty million cable television viewers. Some of the leading companies in this campaign were McDonald's, AFLAC, Atmos Energy, Ashland Oil, Motorola, and Wendy's International. The program was designed to raise awareness about the NAIC and stock ownership in general.

On a more philosophical level, the program exemplifies what the NAIC hopes to instill in its investors. By buying stock, you're contributing to a productive enterprise. That involvement supports economic development, sustains communities, and creates jobs. It's one of the most potent forms of positive reinforcement available to capitalists. The best companies know this and court those who are like minded.

More important, individual owners give a company's shares a degree of stability when times are tough. Since individuals tend to buy and hold stocks for longer periods than institutions, they are less likely to sell during a downturn, earnings surprises (earnings are less than projected by most analysts), or unforeseen developments in the company's industry or markets. DRP plans keep shareholders investing because they can do so on a regular basis with small amounts. It's also easy to see how much their money compounds with dividends and splits.

For example, William Bird, director of investor relations for Kerr-McGee Corp., has found that institutional investors "follow a herd instinct" and sell off without the slightest provocation. So Bird's company recently started a direct investment/DRP for individuals to boost the one-third stake that these investors hold in the company. Although the company absorbs all of the brokerage and administrative costs for the plan, it could pay off for a company like Kerr-McGee, an oil, gas, and coal exploration company whose stock gyrates with the price of these commodities.

The presence of individual investors sustains companies in highly competitive markets through periods of expansion and restructuring. Debbie Mitchell, vice president of investor relations for Wendy's International, likens the small investor stake to "insurance" when the company experiences a downturn.

Another important, though less measurable, element is that stockholders tend to be loyal customers. For a company like Wendy's, battling dozens of competitors lined up right next to each other on commercial strips, the loyalty of customers assures repeat business—and finances future growth.

The unique nature of the individual long-term investor is why more and more corporations are offering DRPs. For investors, there is a relationship between companies that extend themselves to long-term shareholders and performance. Some of the best-performing companies on the market are also top NAIC club holdings. Some of these companies are established concerns like McDonald's, Wal-Mart, PepsiCo, Merck, AT&T, and Philip Morris.

Others, however, are not so well known to most investors but sport impressive records. This group includes AFLAC, RPM, Dana, Cincinnati Bell, Hannaford Brothers, and Biomet. For smaller companies not generally followed by institutions, individual ownership assumes a powerful role. That's why DRPs have become powerful vehicles for amateur investors.

## How DRPs Work

DRPs are to the individual investor what Sears is to power tools. These corporate instruments offer durable, low-cost means to invest with small amounts of money. If you're starting an investment club, DRPs are invaluable for keeping costs down and for dollar-cost averaging.

With most stocks, you can either hold the certificates yourself or in "street name" through a broker. Then you have to deal with small quarterly checks of $12.20 and $16.40 that keep popping up in the mail. DRPs take these dividends and reinvest them automatically on a monthly or quarterly basis in new shares of the company.

DRPs have gotten to be so popular that they are offered by nearly 65 percent of the companies in the Standard & Poor's 500 index. More important, you can invest new money in shares and avoid broker commissions altogether, although 71 percent of companies cover most administrative and brokerage fees, according to Evergreen Enterprises.

Through DRPs, the amount of money you save depends on how much you invest. If you buy one hundred shares of a $50 stock through a broker for a $40 commission (on the buy side), you've spent $5,040 for your purchase. For your tax basis, you subtract the commission from the total cost of the shares. Buying the same amount of shares through a DRP (and perhaps paying a nominal fee of $1) enables you to put nearly all of your money to work.

In addition to no-commission sales, some 20 percent of DRPs offer reinvestment/new purchase of shares at a discount to the market, so you're saving even more. These discounts range from 1 percent to 10 percent. Royce Value Trust, for example, even allows shareholders the right to purchase new shares at a discount to market and to receive dividends in new shares. Although not a full-fledged DRP, plans like these avoid relatively small dividend checks that one is tempted not to reinvest.

Because DRPs are registered in your name, the company holds the shares for you. You don't have to worry about safely storing certificates in a safety-deposit box. Because dividends are invested automatically in new shares, DRPs are one of the best savings plans. If you're a long-term investor, you build your position over time. Stock splits are also recorded automatically, so you don't have to do any additional work to keep track of more (or less, in the case of reverse splits) shares. It's even possible to invest in a portfolio of stocks offering DRPs. Several services such as *Moneypaper* and *DRIP Investor* (see page 171), assemble and monitor the portfolio for you.

Corporations that have run successful DRPs welcome individ-

ual or club investors because they provide an inexpensive source
of capital. It's a much more expensive proposition for companies
to go to banks, float commercial paper, or issue new shares. Why
bother when investors come to you every day and, like clockwork,
keep reinvesting their dividends to buy new shares? Besides, stock
offered directly through companies cuts their administrative
costs.

## DRPs and Growth Stocks

The fact that a handful of companies offering DRPs are also
good growth stocks does not mean all DRP companies are. You
should submit any DRP stock to the rigorous testing described
earlier in this book.

Neither a DRP nor a healthy dividend guarantees a company
is well managed, headed for more growth, or immune to market
pressures. Utilities in particular get battered when interest rates
rise, since these companies' finances are tied to the bond market.
Dividend-rich pharmaceuticals (Lilly, Abbott, Bristol-Myers
Squibb, et al) were drubbed in 1992–94 as the Clinton health
care plan was being promoted. So there are no givens when you
jump into a DRP. A DRP is merely a tool for investing, not a buy
signal.

Within the tight circle of long-term winners, though, some
companies that offer DRPs have been great investments. Rubbermaid is a good case study. The company has launched some
two hundred new products per year for the last several years. This
stunning product cycle has produced impressive earnings and
growth. A $10,000 investment in Rubbermaid made in 1980
would have grown to more than $210,000 by 1990 (although it
stumbled somewhat in 1994). Other brand-name DRPs read like

a *Who's Who* of American corporate success stories. Among them are General Electric, H. J. Heinz, Johnson & Johnson, McDonald's, Merck, 3M, PepsiCo, and Procter & Gamble.

With this select group of growth stocks, a long-term investor reaped great bargains by using DRPs. But the greatest benefits were conferred over time. It's extremely difficult to make a killing in a DRP in a short period of time. In fact, jumping in and out of a plan can be a good way to lose money, since you're likely to guess wrong on the right time to buy and sell.

## Brokers & DRPs

One Chicago-area club ran into a snag concerning a stock that offered a dividend reinvestment plan. They had a difficult time getting information from their broker on how to enroll in the DRP. Since this situation involved a full-service broker, there was little mystery to me. Brokers make money on stock you trade through them, so they have *no interest* in steering you into a DRP. Once you're in a DRP, you're not paying any more commissions, although most plans levy nominal fees. So don't look to your broker for DRP information.

You do need a broker, however, to buy at least one share to qualify for a DRP program. The only exceptions are companies that offer direct-purchase DRPs (such as Exxon, Texaco, Dial) or low-cost programs offered through the NAIC and others; these let you bypass the brokers directly. And when you buy that share from a broker, make sure you pay as little as possible. Brokers will also offer programs that automatically reinvest dividends, but they're not the same as DRP programs offered by companies.

## DRP Drawbacks

Not all DRPs are alike, however. Although most require a one-share balance to open, some may require as many as fifty to one hundred shares. Companies that complained of the costly paperwork to maintain DRPs have raised fees or plan minimums to scare away smaller investors. Bristol-Myers Squibb (listed BMY on the NYSE) is a good example. The drug company was attracting thousands of small investors to its DRP in the early 1990s because its dividend was over 5 percent. In an era of 2.5 percent to 3 percent money market rates, this was a sensational return for a cash-rich, profitable company.

Although the company's stock was pummeled from 1992 to 1994 because of political concerns over the Clinton health care plan (it went from $80 to under $60 a share), it became a haven for bargain-hunting individual investors who could buy shares below $60 and reap the 5 percent–plus yield, which is rare for a nonutility. But when January 1, 1994, rolled along, BMY closed the door on investors who had under fifty shares in the company's DRP. At that time, the company cashed out investors who held shares below the minimum or refused to buy more.

It's too early to tell whether the BMY move was a widespread development in DRPs. BMY is a large company with a considerable institutional following that buys blocks of millions of shares at a time—and promptly dumped the stock when Mrs. Clinton made some disparaging comments about prescription drug prices. Nevertheless, big companies like Texaco and McDonald's welcome individuals with open arms.

Clearly hundreds of smaller companies relish the thought of loyal individual investors who buy shares on a regular basis no matter what the market says the stock is worth that quarter. RPM, the coatings manufacturer, is among this group. The company has openly courted NAIC members and is one of the top holdings of NAIC members.

Here are a few items to watch with DRPs:

• If you're investing small dollars in a DRP, the reinvestment fees can nibble away, although they're much less onerous than commissions. If you're reinvesting $10 per quarter in U.S. West, for example, and get nicked with their $1 reinvestment fee, that's 10 percent of your purchase price. Obviously the more you invest, the more trivial that fee becomes. Moreover, you're still better off in the DRP versus paying a full commission on your new investment or reinvestment.

• Paperwork is also a bugaboo with DRPs. Every single dividend requires a new mailing, even if the dividend is only a few cents. Add in prospectuses, quarterly/annual reports, and other information and you have a small mountain of paperwork. For example, RPM inadvertently created two DRP accounts for my wife and me. This mistake generated months of records that kept accumulating slightly more than two dollars' worth of dividends and fractional shares. Nevertheless, come tax time you'll need these statements to show your buy and sell basis, so you can't throw anything out.

• Another paperwork problem is that you can liquidate your DRP only through written authorization, which is usually a box you check on your quarterly statement. Some DRPs even require signature guarantees, which involves going to a bank or notary public. These transactions often lengthen the time it takes to "cash out" of a DRP—usually from five to ten business days. Although you may own fractional shares, you'll receive a check for the proceeds.

• You have no control over when the company buys or sells its stock, although it does so on a regular basis for all participants in the plan. That's why it pays to dollar-cost average over a long period of time. If you want to sell certain shares at certain times (for tax reasons, such as to avoid high capital gains), instruct the company in writing.

• The most pronounced drawback of DRPs is their absence among the smaller growth companies, especially those listed on the American Stock Exchange and on NASDAQ. That situation, however, is changing as more companies realize the importance of individuals and club investors.

• It's important to note whether a plan allows optional cash payments (OCPs) and partial dividend reinvestment. These options are particularly useful for individuals or clubs. Also ask about reinvestment or selling fees. Keep in mind that some DRPs may charge a small brokerage commission on the sell side.

### Direct-Purchase Stocks

These are the true "free lunch" stocks because they don't even require you to go through a broker. You can buy them directly through the companies. Texaco is the best known of the direct-purchase companies. Others are utility companies that may restrict purchase to residents of a particular state or employees of the company. These are among the best deals in stock purchases, although each company should be considered on its merits, of which the money you'll save on commissions is only one aspect.

These direct-purchase programs are expanding as they become more popular. The best way to find out if they exist is to call the shareholder relations department of the stocks you are considering.

**Direct-Purchase Companies (A Sampling)**

American Recreation (916-852-8005)
Atmos Energy (800-382-8667)
DQE (800-247-0400)
Dial (800-453-2235)
Exxon (800-252-1800)
W. R. Grace (407-362-2000)
SCANA (800-763-5891)
Texaco (800-283-9785)

## HOW TO FIND DIVIDEND DYNAMOS

Since dividend records are public information, they're not hard to find. More often than not it will cost you nothing to research companies through the resources in your public library. When doing so, look for dividend growth—that is, percentage of dividend increases—and if there are consecutive periods of growth. These strings of investor rewards show if a company is a long-distance runner or a sprinter. All of the following sources also rate the company's financial health in addition to dividend growth.

• *Directory of Companies Offering Dividend Reinvestment Plans* (Evergreen Enterprises, P.O. Box 763, Laurel, MD 20725-0763, 301-549-3939). Although this volume is a basic introduction to DRPs, Evergreen also offers DRP portfolio tracking software and a looseleaf service describing DRPs.

• *DRIP Investor* (7412 Calumet Ave., Hammond, IN 46324). The newsletter provides an updated listing of nine hundred companies that offer DRPs plus tips and model portfolios. Also read a copy of the useful book *Buying Stocks Without a Broker*, by newsletter editor Charles Carlson.

• *DRIPsoft* (P.O. Box 169, Oxford, MA 01540). A computer service that provides information on more than 1,400 stocks and closed-end funds. Monthly and quarterly updates are available.

• *First Share* (800-683-0743). For a $12 membership fee, you're entitled to a handbook and the right to buy single shares from other members in a co-op arrangement. You pay the market price of the stock and a suggested $7.50 fee to the other member.

• *Investment Quality Trends* (7440 Girard Ave., Suite #4, La Jolla, CA 92037, 619-459-3818). Publisher Geraldine Weiss is one of the most respected dividend-oriented newsletter advisers in the business. Her rating method is based on the relationship between the stock's dividend yield and stock price. Accordingly, she identifies "blue chips" that may be undervalued because of price dips. She favors a blue chip if

1. the dividend has climbed five times in the last twelve years
2. the company carries an "A" S&P quality rating
3. there are at least five million outstanding shares
4. at least eighty institutional investors are holding the stock
5. the company has posted at least twenty-five years of uninterrupted dividends
6. earnings have risen in seven of the last twelve years

Weiss's method is geared toward safety and dividend growth, so it's worth a look. She also has authored a book—*Dividends Don't Lie*—based on the newsletter. In a world where three out of every four newsletter advisers don't beat the market, Weiss boasts a market-beating return for her portfolio.

• *Moneypaper, the Monthly Guide for the Self-Reliant Investor* (1010 Mamaroneck Ave., Mamaroneck, NY 10543, 800-426-2777). This service combines an investment newsletter and recommended portfolio with a stock purchase plan for 838 companies. A $15 service fee plus the price of the stock and a 10 percent refundable "cushion"—in case the stock moves up or down before the purchase is completed—is charged. Excluding the "cushion" charge, this service charge is roughly half what the lowest discount broker charges. You need to be an owner of record of at least one share of stock in order to participate. Although the newsletter is a bit scattershot, it includes hundreds of recommendations on direct-purchase and dividend reinvestment plan stocks. Some independent commentaries and a "DRP Index" that tracks sixty-three DRP stocks are worthwhile if your portfolio focuses on these kinds of issues. A one-year subscription is $72; two years, $108; three years, $153.

• *Moody's Handbook of Dividend Achievers* ($19.95, Moody's Investor Services, 800-342-5647, ext. 0435, 212-553-0300). This book rates 325 companies that have paid rising dividends over the past ten years. Peter Lynch generously counsels people to "buy stocks from Moody's [Dividend Achievers] list, and stick with them as long as they stay on the list." Some of the stars of this book include companies with forty straight years of dividend growth.

• *NAIC Low-Cost Investment Plan* (711 13-Mile Road, Madison Heights, MI 48071). Offered to club members (individual or

group), the plan was devised to keep the costs of long-term investing to an absolute minimum. So the NAIC negotiated with companies to open up their plans to club members who can buy one
share to gain entry. As with the Moneypaper plan, you pay a $5
onetime setup charge, the cost for the approximate market price
of one share plus an adjustment cost of $10 to cover price fluc-
tuation. Once you're in, all of your paperwork will come from the
company. This generous offering ranges from the well-known
(AT&T, Dow Chemical, Quaker Oats) to small, regional utilities. Once you enroll in the plan, the NAIC deposits your funds
in an escrow account, then transfers it to the company DRPs.
The transactions typically take from six to eight weeks since the
corporations' dividend reinvestment agents must record your
purchases and get your paperwork started. Then your funds can
be invested regularly on a monthly, quarterly, or forty-five-day
period (depending on the plan's rules). You can terminate or
request share certificates at any time. The list of low-cost plan
companies is constantly expanding. For a current list, contact the
NAIC.

• *Charles Schwab DRP Service.* This service is offered mainly as a convenience to clients, as some additional fees are
involved. Although there is no annual fee, you can reinvest dividends on some 3,500 stocks for $0.035 per share, or a $3.50 flat
rate (whichever is less), for dividends under $250; $0.015 per
share for dividends over $250. Unfortunately, if you make addi-
tional cash payments in this plan, you have to pay Schwab's minimum commission. This makes the service a mixed bag, although
it may give you access to a DRP for companies that don't formal-
ly offer one.

• *Standard & Poor's Outlook* (August 25 issue, available in
most libraries). This bedrock of investment newsletters rates

twenty-nine companies that have paid dividends for at least fifty years and increased payments for the last five. Each stock also has a yield matching that of the S&P 500 and is rated highly for other investment characteristics.

# PART IV

# Managing a Growing Portfolio

# CHAPTER 10

## Putting It All Together:
## Quibble & Nibble

The "Quibble & Nibble" (Q&N) club, based in suburban Chicago, has thrived for over twenty-five years by doing its homework. Sitting in on a Q&N meeting, I immediately discovered the reason for their protocol. The entire back of the room was filled with prospective club members, all on a waiting list to join the thirty-member group, which consisted of men in their sixties and seventies. As a test of their eagerness to join, their attendance at meetings was being monitored. Those with the best attendance record would be given an invitation as soon as an opening occurred.

Willis Ranney was more than cordial when I arrived. He introduced me to the group and I sat next to Cliff Merry, the assistant treasurer, who had extended the original invitation. Like most of the rest of the group, Cliff was buried in research paperwork. There was little small talk as Willis launched the group right into the agenda.

The organization of the club was efficient and productive. Four stock-picking committees were entrusted with monitoring existing stocks and finding new ones. Each stock was researched by two members in case one member couldn't make the meeting. The club's portfolio performance was neatly graphed by Cliff, who was one of the many members fluent at computer analyses. The meeting flowed like a corporate affair, only without the padding. Not a single member talked about his golf game.

One by one, the current holdings were reviewed and scrutinized. Then new stocks were put up for consideration: Sears, Airborne Freight, Healthcare Compare, Kellogg, Manitowoc, and Sara Lee. All were tabled for future buys. A motion to buy one hundred shares of Amgen was disapproved by the club's treasury members, who insisted there wasn't enough money. After some discussion of buying less, the motion was tabled.

While the group was happy that it beat the S&P 500 this month and targeted a 15 percent annual average return, there was some discontent about several of the club's newer (losing) holdings in Biomet, Merck, Parametric Technologies, and Sigma-Aldrich. But after reports were read on each, the club settled down and didn't move to sell. Something in the group dynamic made it difficult to unload a losing position that was relatively new. No one in the club wanted to be saddled with picking a loser, and no one wanted to hang that label on their colleagues, either. Besides, like most NAIC clubs, this one preferred to hold if all of the numbers looked favorable and there was no discernible change in management.

Throughout the meeting, Willis was acting as moderator, providing balance as members voiced their concerns on companies that weren't performing well or might be past their prime. When one member noted that Wal-Mart might be running out of gas and motioned to sell a part of their $14,000-plus position, Willis noted, "They're expanding in Canada, Mexico, and Latin America. How big can they get? I don't know."

The most impressive part of the meeting came when Cliff presented his computer printouts. Not only had he monitored the club's portfolio, he'd analyzed upside/downside ratios, S&P ratings, and price/earnings ratios that were below a five-year average.

"Fourteen of sixteen of our stocks are in the buy range," Cliff noted with executive precision. "And ten of sixteen have P/E ratios below the five-year average. They're temporarily depressed and worth buying. A good example is GE, which is solid and has low volatility."

Based on his research, Cliff found that the Q&N portfolio was in good shape and poised for gains if the market didn't head south. They had bought quality, and most wanted to stay the course. He'd also relied upon outside services such as Value Line and S&P to reach his conclusion. As a result, their $200,000-plus portfolio was on a pace for a 30 percent return—in a down market; between November 1994 and April 1995, the club's portfolio went up 20 percent. The club's experiences had made the members' retirements comfortable. They'd all invested in their own portfolios, even if the club had rejected a stock. A sampling of some of the gains they'd racked up by following their numbers over the past twenty-five years included the following:

| Stock | $ Gain |
| --- | --- |
| Abbott Labs | $21,169 |
| Newell | $16,361 |
| Procter & Gamble | $20,449 |
| Walgreen's | $9,650 |
| Wal-Mart | $2,485 |

*Note: Portfolio gains as of 6/3/94. Stock splits or dividend income not reflected.*

---

Investfact: If you had put $1,000 into the S&P 500 index on January 31, 1940, and left it there for fifty-two years, you'd have $333,793 through 1992. If you'd added $1,000 a year every January for fifty-two years, your initial $52,000 investment would be worth $3,554,227. This illustrates the importance of buying, holding, and compounding.

Source: Peter Lynch, *Beating the Street*

---

## WHAT MAKES A WINNER?

By now you've probably gleaned that long-term winners have a penchant for top-flight management that produces consistent earnings and sales growth. There's a direct correlation between the most growth-oriented companies and the widest holdings of the NAIC members. Every year since 1984, *Better Investing* has surveyed NAIC members to determine the most widely held stocks. The most popular stocks may not be the most successful, but none of them are laggards. The following list is a profile of stocks that have appeared on the list's top ten ranking more than half the time.

| Stock | Industry | DRP | DDG | GAM | Foreign Sales |
|-------|----------|-----|-----|-----|---------------|
| McDonald's | Food | Y | Y | Y | Y |
| AT&T | Telecommunications | Y | Y | Y | Y |
| AFLAC | Insurance | Y | Y | Y | Y |

| PepsiCo | Food | Y | Y | Y | Y |
|---------|------|---|---|---|---|
| Disney | Entertainment | N | Y | Y | Y |
| Abbott Labs | Health | Y | Y | Y | Y |
| Wal-Mart | Retail | Y | Y | Y | Y |

Note: DRP = *dividend reinvestment plan*; GAM = *growth-oriented management*; DDG = *double-digit earnings, or sales growth*.

It's also no coincidence that these stocks frequently appear in the best "All-Star" portfolios, mostly because of their consistency in boosting earnings and sales.

Companies that dropped off the list are notable for what they didn't do: keep up with industry changes and enhance their market position. For example, one of the most popular stocks in 1984 was IBM, then the darling of individuals, clubs, and institutions alike. This was a company that did everything right—except keep up with changes in the computer business. Now, having gone through a wrenching restructuring, massive layoffs, and new management, it still may not be down for the count.

Those companies that kept pace with their industries and continued to grow were held for tidy profits. A snapshot of popular stocks in "All-Star" portfolios of 1985 shows the presence of Abbott, AT&T, McDonald's, GE, and AFLAC.

It helps to get in on a good stock before the rest of the world discovers it. McDonald's was in some of the top portfolios in 1985 but ranked only sixty-sixth on the NAIC's list of most widely held stocks. It has since jumped to the top spot (as of the 1993 poll). Will these stocks continue to show robust growth? Only constant monitoring will tell. One trend, however, is certain to continue, barring a cataclysm in the stock market. More individuals will become stock investors. Largely as a result of paltry savings yields and the NAIC's success in recruiting corporate sponsorship through its "Own a Share in America" program, more than 20 million individuals now own stock, up from 6.5 million in the 1950s.

> Investfact: Post–World War II bear markets have an average life span of thirty-three months. The longest bull market to date was August 1982 through August 1987, a time of generally declining interest rates.

## MARKET TIMING

The seven members of the Stock Barons club, meeting in Des Plaines, Illinois, were pondering whether they should sell Sara Lee. The club was concerned that "Sara's" high-profile chairman, John Bryan, was dabbling too much in Democratic Party affairs and that the company's management might be rudderless. In the basement of a tidy tract home, the discussion became turbulent. The monthly meeting then plunged into its regular "portfolio review," a staple of every organized club's agenda.

The Barons' Sara Lee investment was down some 32 percent since they'd bought in February 1992. Although they only owned fifty-four shares, they were as concerned as someone owning one million shares. Members were getting edgy and were wondering if they should sell. Velma, retired, and one of the oldest club members, peered through her glasses at the other members as the debate picked up.

"You know, I heard a rumor on Channel Twenty-six [a local television financial program] that Sara Lee might merge with Philip Morris. A lot of people like the idea of Sara and Philip getting married," she said, chuckling.

Since the club also owned Philip Morris—and had seen *that*

position plummet by one-third—Velma's rumor was exciting but prompted only more questions. Following the conventional wisdom, thousands of clubs, individuals, and institutions bought Philip Morris, thought to be a "bulletproof" company because of its dominant position in the recession-proof food, beverage, and tobacco industries. It also offered a healthy dividend and steady earnings. But when Wall Street sold off "name-brand" companies in late 1993 (like PM) and Congress inflamed the public health/tobacco issue, Philip Morris took a dive.

Mary, who led the charge on Sara's management woes, noted that the company had a shake-up in its European divisions. Poking into *Value Line*, members observed that this was a critical area for Sara, since 38 percent of its earnings come from foreign operations.

"That's right," retorted Arlene, who had seen lots of managements come and go in her twenty years as an individual investor. "If you have a problem with management, it can take up to two years before it [earnings growth] comes back," she offered with authority.

Velma weighed in again with the fact that Sara was among a "top-notch group of food companies." (The corporation also sells Hanes underwear, Hillshire sausage, Playtex bras, Isotoner gloves, and Coach bags and purses.)

"Coach products are good; some of them cost hundreds of dollars," opined Bernice, looking down through her half-specs. Bernice was a key member because she owned the *Value Line* survey subscription and was attending with her businessman son, Harlan.

"I have a Coach *key chain*," Velma quipped sardonically, to the laughter of club members, which released the tension.

Harlan, trying to flesh out the Sara issue to another level, opened up the *Value Line* survey and read the report. The stock rating service predicted that the company would return to "double-digit growth." The discussion abated and Tony, the president, moved the club onto Wal-Mart and presentations on four new stocks that Mike and Bernice had researched.

Although the Stock Barons had rung up impressive gains in AFLAC (up 245 percent), McDonald's (up 175 percent), and Blockbuster (up 112 percent), they were caught in the doldrums with other former highfliers. Merck, Abbott Labs, Browning-Ferris, and Safety-Kleen were once the premier growth stocks of the early 1990s. But health care reform, changing industries, and a recession had beaten them down six percent to 43 percent. The club was unsure whether to unload the stocks or wait out the spate of bad news that had plagued these companies. The club discussed each one of the stocks, reading out loud recent newspaper articles. They all reached the same conclusion by default: hold.

Like most established clubs, the Stock Barons had "run the numbers," carefully examining earnings/share, management, profit projections, and *Value Line* analyses. This was standard operating procedure, performed tens of thousands of times when clubs dissected stocks using the NAIC's *Stock Selection Guide*. What perplexed the Barons—and thousands of other clubs—was where their stocks stood relative to the current phase of the market. Were they still good companies, or were other temporary factors at play? Investment advice sources were good at evaluating stocks to buy but light on when to sell.

The Barons had had some experience with the market's fits and turns, and as a result they believed in patience. According to Arlene, the club started in 1986 and did well up until October 19, 1987, when the market nosedived Black Monday. While she says the club "lost everything" after the crash, they've stayed the course. It's been rewarding, since their average position has gained 76 percent. Nevertheless, the nagging question on when to sell and when to ride out "the unseen hand" of a market cycle weighs heavily on lots of investors like the Barons.

Not long after I met with the Barons, Sara Lee announced a massive restructuring. Chairman Bryan says he will not only cut 8,500 jobs, but will curb acquisitions to beef up returns. Sara's stock price perked up after the move.

## MARKET CYCLES

It's safe to say that most individual and club investors are "bottom up" investors. This misleading bit of financial jargon doesn't mean that a stock is sunk to the bottom of the ocean before it's bought. It refers to judging each company by its merits (balance sheet, management, and so forth) and not by the state of the economy or business cycles. Those who preach "top down" stock picking are constantly reading statistics and graphs and holding their breath until the government releases another report on the state of the economy. Certainly government indicators have some impact on the market, but it's nearly impossible to invest based on a vague set of numbers that few people understand.

The study of market, business, and economic cycles has preoccupied academics, financiers, and economists for more than 250 years. From Adam Smith to Arthur Laffer, the investing public has displayed an inordinate amount of interest in the obscure snapshots of the "big picture." Unfortunately for most investors, the big picture is a blur to most and confers few bragging rights to all but the most overpaid economists and analysts.

Knowing how cycles move the market, however, can give you some insights on when to buy and sell. Although it's an imprecise business, catching the cycle at the right time can definitely mean the difference between buying low and selling high—and when not to do so.

If you listen to the financial news on a regular basis, you know how crazy this subject can get. Every expert is constantly trying to guess where the economy is going at any particular moment. The problem is, there are many separate economies moving in different directions. So when an economist says that the "economy is moving up," it's practically meaningless because of the different aspects of business cycles. Individual and club investors need to watch many trends to give them some perspective. Following are the major factors to keep an eye on. You can chart business cycles by tracking government statistics, reading business newspapers or magazines, or listening to the radio or watching business TV shows.

## Interest Rate/Inflation Cycles

This is one of the biggest engines of growth or decline. When rates are moving up, they can kill off demand for goods and services. When rates decline, financial companies, utilities, and any number of other industries can prosper because their cost of doing business is down. Inflation is directly related to interest rates. Practically the only vehicles that prosper in inflationary times are "hard assets" such as gold, silver, commodities, and real estate. Inflation robs most owners of financial (stocks, bonds, money market/savings vehicles) assets of real return, which is the return minus inflation. Indicators like retail, auto, housing, and factory orders are often a result of swings in interest rates and inflation.

Interest rates and inflation typically move in lockstep, although not always, as proved by the Federal Reserve Bank's reaction to "phantom" inflation in 1993–94. Inflation, which refers to upward movement of prices in goods and services, determines how much things cost. If wages go up, company operating costs rise. If jet fuel goes up, airline tickets may cost more and airline profits drop. If bread costs more because of a bad wheat crop caused by a midwest drought, then we all pay more at the supermarket. These are examples of how the Commerce Department defines our "cost of living." The Commerce Department monitors two components of inflation:

• *The producer price index (PPI)*. This is largely inflation at the wholesale level. Depending upon the overall economy, particular industries, and business competition, these prices may or may not be passed on to consumers. A rise in this index shows that businesses are raising prices for what they sell. This is a problem only if the PPI translates into a rise in the consumer price index. So keep an eye on consumer prices when a rising PPI is announced.

• *The consumer price index (CPI)*. This represents a breadbasket of one hundred thousand goods and services that most consumers buy. The major components are food and energy. Also included are seasonally impacted items such as autos, housing starts, and clothing. The CPI is a big number to watch since it reflects the overall cost of living. The Federal Reserve uses it as benchmark to determine whether interest rates should rise to contain inflation (by restricting credit) or be lowered to permit expansion (by loosening credit). Since wages, Social Security increases, and pensions are tied to the CPI, just about everything costs more if the CPI rises. Any rate of increase below 4 percent is considered low to moderate. Anything above 5 percent is worrisome. Double-digit CPI increases spell trouble for stocks. However, they translate into another heyday in real estate, precious metals, and other "hard asset" commodities. If that's the case, welcome back to the 1970s and the days of rampant real estate speculation and 14 percent money market accounts. Falling interest rates are generally good for the economy and bode particularly well for interest-driven concerns like banks, savings and loans, utilities, and insurers.

If you recall the *Wizard of Oz*, I'd like to point your attention to the "man behind the curtain" in this interest rate/inflation journey. In this case it's the Federal Reserve System, which controls the flow of money throughout the U.S. and the international banking system. The "Fed" has the power to control inflation *and* interest rates by restricting the flow of credit and pumping money into the banking system (the money supply). The Fed does this through buying and selling U.S. government securities and tinkering with their "discount" and "federal funds" rates. These are rates on short-term and overnight loans within the Federal Reserve System. Although you and I can't get these rock-bottom loan rates, what big money center banks like Bank of America, Citibank, and First Chicago pay on interest dictates what we pay and how much corporate America pays. These rates are usually based on the CPI: the higher the inflation, the higher the rates. In fact, the federal discount rate is usually within one point of the consumer price index.

The Fed, a huge money pump, directly and indirectly determines how much Treasury bills, notes, and bonds pay in interest, how much home-equity loans cost, and how much corporations pay to finance new equipment (capital goods). So when the Fed moves, the markets quake. Even modest rumors turn the market upside down. Interest rate upticks usually beat up stocks. One exception is when the market thinks that rate hikes are designed to curb inflation, which is the enemy of most corporations.

As a quasi-public institution, the Fed acts independently. It's supervised by neither Congress nor the U.S. Treasury. The Fed was set up to be a "bank of banks"—that is, connected directly to banks and not to the average citizen. It also serves as lender of last resort when money center banks or the stock markets find themselves in a cash crunch. When Continental Illinois Bank of Chicago had a massive run on deposits in the early 1980s, the Fed had to bail it out. Since it was linked to the international banking system, Continental's collapse would certainly have triggered an international banking debacle—and worldwide depression. The Fed also pulled its lifeboat of cash alongside the New York Stock Exchange in late 1987 when the market crashed five hundred points. The Fed likes to keep the big boys liquid. When it whispers, Wall Street roars.

It's no secret that the Fed's reins on the money supply and interest rates can create recessions as well as upturns. The wrenching contraction of credit in the late 1970s and early 1980s forced the world into a recession, which was largely induced by Fed chief Paul Volcker's contraction of credit and interest rates. This draconian move, however, is believed to have halted the double-digit inflation that ravaged Western economies throughout the 1970s.

The Fed's business is to keep inflation in check when it isn't policing the banking system. Surges of inflation may push rates higher, which signals the beginning and end of a business cycle. Nearly every industry is impacted by these cycles. Corporate activities follow these cycles because they must adjust to supply and demand and the costs of borrowing for expansion. If interest rates are rising and the economy is contracting, then their profits may decline. It all depends on the kind of business cycle that flows from the movement of interest rates and inflation.

## Manufacturers' New Orders

This represents new business and how well situated industry is for the future. Most manufacturers gauge the growth of their businesses by how many new orders (durable goods, inventories, and so on) they have "booked." Inventories reflect how much of their product they have on hand to sell. Although this can be interpreted many ways, it's a good sign if manufacturers have adequate inventory to meet current and future demand. Excessive inventory in times of slack demand cuts into profits. For example, if automakers overproduce a certain vehicle and inventories build up, then that will cut into profits if demand doesn't pick up. You can also check a company's inventory and order status in its annual report.

## Industrial Production and Capacity Utilization, Purchasing Manager's Index

These indicators show overall rates of industrial activity. If factories are running at or near capacity, that means business is good. A downturn spells a declining cycle. Heavy industries often post their best profits when they are running their plants near full capacity. Even better yet, if they're building new factories, they're expanding their business. The purchasing manager's index reflects how much business is buying in terms of capital goods and supplies to sustain operations. If purchasing managers are more active, then industrial activity is on the upswing.

## Retail Sales, Housing Starts, Auto Sales

These are critical numbers when gauging the consumer economy. All of these numbers are relatively depressed during recessions. They also have specific implications for certain industries. When housing starts are up, for example, there's a good demand for building products and mortgages. As a result, banks, thrifts, and building products companies thrive. Coming out of a recession, this troika shows a rebound. The opposite is true on the way down. The Wal-Marts, Kmarts, Searses, and Limiteds of the world feel these numbers most directly. The market favors companies (as a group and individually) that are on the leading edge of a business cycle.

## Consumer Confidence, Installment Credit, Personal Income

If consumers have money to spend, they'll spend it and use credit. These numbers bode well for most retail businesses. If consumers aren't confident, they won't be buying clothes, cars, or boats, taking vacations, or going to casinos. People out of work or fearing layoffs don't spend money on the two-thirds of the economy that caters to consumers.

## Gross Domestic Product, Index of Leading Economic Indicators, Employment/Unemployment

These are some more "big numbers" that attempt to show where the total of goods and services is going. Increases generally show expansion. Declines (of three months or more) signal recessions. These are very broad guidelines that can be used in conjunction with the other figures. Business cycles go from troughs to peaks based on what's reflected in these numbers. It's a bad time to invest if the trend is down, unless you plan to hold on throughout the entire cycle. The bond market, which triggers moves in the stock market, keys off of unemployment figures (in addition to interest rates and inflation). Surges in employment may signal inflation, which is a negative for both stocks and bonds. It's a fickle set of numbers, difficult to interpret in terms of a single company or industry.

## Industrial Cycles

Manufacturing of autos, chemicals, paper, and various technologies have their own cycles. In a recession, though, these cycles tend to be in a trough because demand is slack. Stocks that ebb and flow in these cycles are called "cyclical" companies.

## Foreign Investment Cycles

With the liberalization of markets in Asia and Latin America, hundreds of billions of dollars from the industrialized world have been flowing into less developed countries. When the spigot gets turned off, however, these markets experience huge contractions (see section on overseas stocks, page 152).

## Natural Resource Cycles

When there's a glut of oil or natural gas, oil prices tend to stay low. When energy prices are low, inflation and interest rates tend to stay low. But any company dependent upon natural resources for its profits is always a hostage to these cycles. Oil, gas, coal, copper, aluminum, steel, and any company that does mining or processing of minerals or natural resources is impacted heavily. Remember that resource prices are one of the main "drivers" behind inflation. Generally, any company involved in these commodities (including agricultural concerns hit by weather problems) is impacted by these cycles.

### Small-Cap Stocks

Stocks with market capitalizations under $1 billion move independently of their blue-chip brethren (see section on small stocks, page 146).

When it comes to the stocks you're considering, though, you have to look at microeconomies versus the macroeconomy of a country or region. Is the company impacted by the above-named cycles? Is it doing business in countries or regions that are in an upswing economically?

## THE DOW 30 MARKET INDEX AND CYCLES

You can't escape it. The Dow Jones Industrial Average is reported hourly and at the close. It's ironic that the mainstream media has latched on to this index since it represents just a small slice of the economy and the world of international business. Keeping in mind that the Dow reflects a small portion of the stock market, you need some insight as to what this number means and how other indexes and cycles are also important for stock picking.

The Dow's popularity used to reflect some cross section of American business. But since the global marketplace has expanded and new industries have been created (such as biotechnology and microcomputers), the Dow is mostly out of step with some of the most vibrant sectors of the economy. Here's the list of companies constituting the elite Dow 30 industrials:

| | |
|---|---|
| Alcoa | Goodyear |
| Allied Signal | IBM |
| American Express | International Paper |
| AT&T | McDonald's |
| Bethlehem Steel | Merck |
| Boeing | 3M |
| Caterpillar | J. P. Morgan |
| Chevron | Philip Morris |
| Coca-Cola | Procter & Gamble |
| Disney | Sears |
| E. I. du Pont | Texaco |
| Eastman Kodak | Union Carbide |
| Exxon | United Technologies |
| General Electric | Westinghouse Electric |
| General Motors | Woolworth |

As you can note from the list, the Dow is notorious for what it *doesn't* include. Where are the high-technology leaders like Microsoft and Novell? Where is the top retailer Wal-Mart? With the exception of McDonald's, where are the service companies? What about the insurance, semiconductor, and communications industries? What about companies with sales under $1 billion? Some of the companies—like Westinghouse, Bethlehem Steel, and American Express—have had some real problems justifying their existence on the Dow. Yet this is the number that causes investors to panic, jump for joy, and reach for the phone to call the broker.

The Dow 30 may be an exclusive club, but it still manages to serve as a reliable indicator of cycles. Most of the companies on the Dow are influenced by business cycles that move in tandem with the economy. Alcoa, for example, does well during economic upturns. As an aluminum producer, the company makes a basic metal for industrial and consumer applications. It typically doesn't do well during recessions when industry doesn't demand as much aluminum. The same can be said for Bethlehem Steel, International Paper, Union Carbide, Boeing, Caterpillar, and du Pont. Basic industries like metals, chemicals, paper, and capital goods (machines that make other things) surge when the GDP and industrial production are growing. While these companies and the Dow 30 used to be the bastion of American industry, they are now merely good heralds for the heavy industrial economy that is less and less a part of the overall global economy.

Of course, it's not a bad idea to pick a stock when it's going up, but it may not be a good time to get the best price. In the face of numerous interpretations applicable to using the Dow averages (the Dow theory) to pick stocks, remember this simple rule:

*Buy when the news is bad and the company is good.*

This is a variation on "buy low, sell high," but it involves a little more analysis. One Dow 30 theory proves itself over and over: If you buy a Dow stock when it's out of favor (declining price) and management restructures the company at its nadir, you'll make more money than if you constantly buy the most popular Dow stocks.

Research has shown that if you buy the lowest-returning and highest-yielding stocks of the Dow 30 and hold for a year, you'll outperform the leading Dow stocks every time. In 1993 this strategy yielded a 27.3 percent total return. It's a twist on Bernard Baruch's "buy when there's blood in the streets" maxim—and one that works with other stocks outside the Dow universe, given that you are also buying valuable companies with sound management and good prospects for growth.

For example, when Sears ran into management problems in recent years, its stock got battered. Then activist shareholders put pressure on Sears's boardroom to restructure and modernize the company. As a result, the behemoth closed its unprofitable catalog, reshaped its retail operations, and sold off its Dean Witter and Allstate subsidiaries. The result was a profitable and robustly competitive Sears, transformed from the jungle of moribund soft goods and hardware. Soft goods were realigned to compete with Sears's leaner and snappier specialty competitors. Appliances were sold on a par with the growing legion of aggressive appliance superstores. But stockholders who bought Sears at sixty didn't make nearly as much money as those who grabbed the bruised company at thirty-eight.

The Sears story is far from over, as the one hundred-year-old company must gear up for the next century of intense competition. Since most of Sears's business (in sales) came from the retail sector, it was wise to buy the company's stock during a recession, when big shareholders were forcing a restructuring. But for savvy investors, the Sears saga is a classic exercise in buying value at the bottom of a business cycle and making money as the economy and company recover.


## THE "WORST TO FIRST" CYCLE

Sometimes you don't even have to pick a company to take advantage of a cycle. Pick a company within an industry or industry sector. As previously mentioned, if you're buying quality when a market cycle is downtrending, you can obtain a better price. "This "worst to first" strategy pays off if you do your homework.

Morningstar Mutual Funds has done some interesting research to prove this phenomenon. The research examined what would happen if you invested in the most out-of-favor categories of stocks from 1970 through 1993 (this means you ignored the hottest kinds of stocks and opted for the lower-performing types). Morningstar found that for 60 percent of the time, the tactic produced better returns than did holding the top- or middle-performing asset class.

"Furthermore," states Morningstar editor John Rekenthaler, "because the best gains were registered by bottom performers rebounding to the top, the contrarian strategy looked even better when aggregate returns were computed: the strategy's 20.24 percent annual rate of return—that is, the average for all asset types over all of the rolling periods—better by nearly 4 percent, and handily beat any of the individual rates of returns for the three asset classes."

As the Bible tells us, "The first shall be last, and the last first." So it goes for betting on cycles turning losers into winners.

## DEMOGRAPHIC CYCLES

This cycle profiles population groups and how they may respond to certain products. For example, the long-term demographic cycle of the United States, Europe, and Japan is toward an older population. Older populations tend to buy more pharmaceutical and travel products and services. This is an involved subject that is becoming a science. It's a key to marketing consumer products.

For example, American Greetings noted in a presentation at an investment fair that prime markets for their products are aging baby boomers and the over-fifty-five market.

"The impact of this aging evolution on American Greetings is profound because older consumers make the most money of any age group, and they spend it on consumer goods that meet their specific needs and lifestyles."

Quality companies know demographic trends and how to market accordingly. Look for this information in the annual report.

## HOW CYCLES IMPACT COMPANIES

Every company reacts differently to business cycles. Some corporations, said to be *defensive*, can hold their own or thrive in downturns. These are usually concerns that consumers and other businesses will patronize no matter what the economy is doing. They are typically clustered in the food, beverage, health care, and entertainment industries. Companies typically described as *cyclical*—those most vulnerable during economic downturns— are clustered within the basic industries that make steel, autos, chemicals, homes, airplanes, luxury items, and environmental equipment. The following list, prepared by Smith Barney Shearson and Standard & Poor's, gives a good idea of the kind of industries that are considered defensive in the face of interest rate hikes.

| Defensive | Cyclical |
|---|---|
| Cosmetics | Aluminum |
| Regional Banks | Housewares |

| | |
|---|---|
| Alcoholic Beverages | Pollution/Environmental |
| Engineering | Home Construction |
| Clothing Manufacture | Airlines |
| Supermarket Chains | Hotels |
| Drugstores | Chemicals/Pharmaceuticals |

**Average Gain/Loss Range During Interest Rate Rise:**

| | |
|---|---|
| +2% to 10% | -34% to -16% |

As you can see, the *industry sector* a company is in can affect a company's price as much as or more than other factors. Notice the inclusion of pharmaceuticals and pollution/environmental on the right side of the table. It's easy to see why the Stock Barons' Merck, Abbott, and Safety-Kleen holdings are struggling, given the sectors they fall into.

There are other reasons why these stocks are depressed, of course. But when the market cycles against your picks, you either backpedal or buy more if you're convinced of a company's quality and management. One great example is Chrysler, which looked as if it were on the ropes in the early 1980s. Its product line was outdated, its plants old, and its sales ravaged by recession. Nevertheless, Lee Iacocca was running the show and had some plans for the future. After he secured a government loan to tide the company over, things began to happen. He revamped the firm's entire product line, cooking up plans for what later became the minivan, and started investing heavily in research and development.

Iacocca's work attracted the notice of Peter Lynch at the Fidelity Magellan fund, who bought huge blocks of Chrysler when the business cycle—and the rest of the world—thought it was a sucker's bet. The result was one of the most dramatic turnarounds in the history of American industry. Iacocca paid back the government loan with interest and (a few popular commercials and best-selling books later) became a folk hero.

So cycles can create some buying opportunities. Let's say that inflation is returning as a scourge on the economy. Are the defensive sectors the same then? With the exception of food, supermarkets, drugstores, and hospitals, this picture changes. Real inflation begets a market run to hard assets and commodities. In this scenario, the sectors that do well include

**Inflationary Defensive Sectors**
Oil and Gas Drilling
Oil Equipment/Service
Natural Resources Conglomerates (Exxon, Shell, Chevron, and so on)
Mining (Basic and Precious Metals)
Real Estate Development and Management
Real Estate Investment Trusts
Agricultural Processors

**Cyclical Industries/Sectors**
Advertising and Marketing Services
Aerospace
Airlines
Aluminum
Banking (Financial Services)
Broadcast Media
Capital Goods (Machine Tools and Manufacturing Equipment)
Communications
Commodity and Specialty Chemicals
Commercial (Business-to-Business) Services

Computers (Hardware and Software)
Electrical Components

**Highly Cyclical**
Environmental Services (Cleanup, Recycling, Remediation)
Forest Products/Paper/Packaging
Home Construction (Building Materials, Contractor Services)
Insurance
Mining and Metals
Real Estate
Steel (Manufacturing, Processing, Fabricating, and Alloys)
Oil Drilling, Refining, Equipment, and Pipelines
Railroads
Retailers
Technology
Trucking
Utilities
Vehicle Manufacturing

**Cyclical Companies**
American Air (AAR)
Boise Cascade (paper)
Caterpillar
Chrysler
Dow Chemical
Ford
GM
W. R. Grace (chemicals)
Maytag
USX Marathon (energy)

## EXCEPTIONS TO THE RULES

As many investment clubbers have discovered, some safe havens aren't what they used to be. First there was the battering of all name-brand food and beverage companies in 1993 because of the recession and a trend away from premium pricing. Then came the shocker: Utilities got hit badly. From December 12, 1991, through May 13, 1994, the Dow Jones Utilities Average plunged nearly 20 percent. Only a small part of that period did the traditional nemesis of utilities emerge—rising interest rates. Since utilities are interest sensitive, they move with bonds. They are so closely connected to the debt securities markets for financing capital improvements that any uptick in rates hurts their cash flow.

Utilities are also in the throes of writing down the costs of expensive nuclear power plants and facing up to a newly deregulated world in which they don't hold monopolies. A big utility customer in New York, for example, can now buy power from utilities in Canada or Ohio.

In the telephone business, cable and other telecommunications services are competing with AT&T and the "Baby Bells" (NYNEX, Ameritech, U.S. West, et al) for a whole range of multimedia superhighway services. Any industry that passes into a wave of technological innovation triggers an entirely new business cycle unique to a particular industry. Such cycles are on the upswing in microcomputers, software, biotechnology, and pharmaceuticals. It pays to do some research to get ahead of the curve of these cycles.

Certain industries also have cycles of their own. Most technology companies have product cycles. Semiconductor firms, for example, have tight cycles for new "chips" they develop. They are good in the marketplace for only so long before they have to move from premium to commodity pricing as newer, faster chips become available. Large capital goods companies are also subject to swings in foreign currencies. A company like Caterpillar, for example, is especially hostage to the yen-dollar relationship since their main competition is in Japan. A modest swing on the foreign currency exchange makes their product pricing more competitive overnight.

Generally, when judging what cycles impact a company's bottom line, look at its different lines of business. Annual reports should be the best resource on this account. Some product "niches" are less prone to cycles than others.

## IMPORTANT INDEXES FOR CYCLE TRACKERS

You can often use indexes to track cycles in certain industries. Although most industries are hurt in a bear market or recession, some do better than others when a recovery is due. For small-capitalization market cycles (companies under $1 billion in sales), the AMEX, NASDAQ, and Russell 2000 indexes are useful to follow.

As a rule, if you want to compare "apples to apples"—that is, similar companies within an industry—check their annual returns against a relevant index. The Dow Utilities Index is most useful for big utility stocks, for example. For large stocks as a group, check the S&P 500. Indexes within a sector are the numbers to beat.

The following are the most widely tracked indexes and what they reflect.

## Dow Jones Averages

Industrials (thirty heavy industry, cyclical companies; see page 194)

Transportation (cross section of railroad, air, and trucking) includes AMR, Airborne Freight, Alaska Air, American President, Burlington Northern, CSX, Carolina Freight, Consolidated Freight, Conrail, Delta Air, Federal Express, Norfolk Southern, Roadway Systems, Ryder Systems, Santa Fe Pacific, Southwest Air, UAL (United Air), USAir, Union Pacific, and XTRA

## Utilities

Major electric and gas utility companies, which include American Electric Power, ArkLa, Centerior Energy, Commonwealth Edison, Consolidated Edison, Consolidated Natural Gas, Detroit Edison, Houston Industries, Niagra Mohawk, Pacific Gas & Electric, Panhandle Eastern, Peco, Peoples Energy, Public Service Ent., and SCECorp

## Dow Jones Composite

A combination of the above industries and companies.

## Standard & Poor's

Similar to Dow Jones, only a broader and different set of companies. Note that the S&P 500 is the widely accepted benchmark for money managers defining the market. This is the index to beat or equal when evaluating a portfolio of large stocks.

Industrial, Transportation, Utilities, Financial, Mid-Cap (medium-size corporations) 400, 500 stocks (largest industrial companies)

## Low-Priced Index

This is a good place to find bargains, according to renowned stock picker Richard Evans, author of *Finding Winners*. Over twenty years, this index has outperformed the S&P 500 index by nearly two to one.

## New York Stock Exchange

For issues listed on this exchange only.

Composite, Industrial, Transportation, Utility, and Finance

## NASDAQ

An electronic exchange consisting of mostly midsize to smaller companies.

Composite, Industrials, Financial, Banks, Insurance

## AMEX (American Stock Exchange)

## RUSSELL 2000

Smaller-capitalization companies.

## Value Line

Companies rated by Value Line.

**Wilshire 5000**

Combines stocks from every exchange.

If you want just a snapshot of what industry group is hot and what's not, turn to the "Dow Jones Industry Groups" box in Section C of *The Wall Street Journal*. This useful little snippet shows you the leading and lagging groups and the strongest stocks that are price leaders in these categories.

For example, the leading groups in mid-May 1994 were precious metals, mining and oil field equipment/drilling/services. The laggards were casinos, heavy machinery, computers, and airlines. You want bargains? Do your homework.

## SHOULD YOU TIME THE MARKET BASED ON CYCLES AND INDEXES?

In a word, no. Why? Because you can guess wrong and still be right if you're buying quality companies. Let's say you had the bad fortune of buying at the worst possible time in a cycle. In this case, it would be when the S&P 500 was at an all-time high for a given year, then immediately retreated.

If you'd invested $2,000 every year on this date from 1973 through 1993, you'd still have $204,734 at the end of the period, netting a *profit* of $162,734. How can you make money even if you guess wrong on *every* single yearly market cycle? The market always bounces back, always makes money long term and favors those who buy and hold—and keep buying more. This single most important truth of stock market investing is confirmed over and over again by Ibbotson Associates research. Stocks lost money in only two of fifty-eight different ten-year holding periods and none in twenty-five-year periods. You also get superior returns that beat inflation.

Even if you had the misfortune to get caught in a bear market, your buy-and-hold strategy guarantees profitability. There have been thirty bear markets since 1900, roughly one every three years. Each bear is followed by a bull, however. There have been eleven bull markets since 1956 alone in which principal gains ranged from 50 percent to 250 percent during those periods. And adjusted for that all-important inflation (you always have to beat it if you want to get ahead), stocks averaged 7 percent in the 1972–91 period versus a paltry 1.5 percent for U.S. Treasury bills.

## MARKET CYCLES AND P/E RATIOS

Volumes have been written on the importance of P/E ratios. Some companies may have had nosebleed P/E's in the 1980s because heavy growth has pushed up the price. Some stocks just become the darlings of analysts and institutions. Witness the pop-

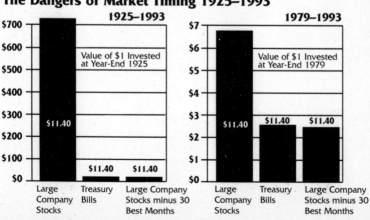

**The Dangers of Market Timing 1925–1993**

ularity of Home Depot, Wal-Mart, Microsoft, and Toys "R" Us in the 1990s. If these companies keep growing, then high P/E's are not a negative factor. Things change with business cycles.

One need only look at biotechnology stocks to see how P/E's move with the market's whim. One year they're filet mignon; the next year they're dog meat. At the first signs of trouble (in terms of a business cycle), most technology stocks are dumped by institutional investors. For this industry sector, P/E's reflect optimism and investors bidding up prices. They contract when the optimism recedes. If you apply your tests of management quality and where a company stands in a business cycle, buying when P/E's are lower may offer you a better price.

A good example is a high-quality stock like Merck, which during the height of its popularity in 1992 sported a P/E of 22.9. In mid-1994, perhaps at its nadir, the stock posted a P/E of 17. Assuming all other factors are equal from both points in time (management, product demand, and so on), Merck is a much better buy at the lower P/E.

To know where you stand on P/E's, always check a company's P/E versus the S&P 500's P/E and the industry average; these numbers are available in *The Wall Street Journal* and *Value Line* survey. As a long-term investor, however, you need to consider management factors as well.

# CHAPTER 11

# It's Not *All* in the Timing

Nothing is more aggravating to an investor than buying a stock for all the right reasons and then selling it off when it fails to perform—only to see it rebound and post a double-digit recovery. It's the bane of every investor's existence.

The fourteen-member Mutual Investment Club of the North Shore, which survived its first trial by fire in the 1987–88 period (when it first started up), were meeting to spruce up its portfolio and consider selling its laggards.

Four out of the ten stocks it held were either marginal or losing money (at the time this was written). Three of those—Abbott Labs, ConAgra, and Sara Lee—had been widely held to be "bulletproof." In conventional Wall Street wisdom, these are defensive companies that supposedly outlast bear markets, business cycles, and political uncertainty. People need medicine and food and buy them no matter how murky the economic climate looks. So the Mutual members were puzzled at the lackluster performance.

Consisting mostly of retired teachers from Chicago's North

Shore suburbs, the club met over cake and coffee in the bright sunroom of Virginia Merry's elegant English-style home. Although Virginia's husband, Cliff, was also an NAIC member, he belonged to another club ("Quibble & Nibble"). The only man attending the meeting—Pierre—was a former bank analyst and author. He was attending with his wife, Binnie.

Charlotte, the group's president, initiated the club's portfolio review, the meat and potatoes of club meetings from coast to coast. After reports were read on Abbott Labs, ConAgra, McDonald's, Motorola, and Pennsylvania Power & Light, the club headed into uncharted territory. Their largest holding—Service Master (225 shares)—was about to convert from a limited partnership to a corporation. Every member wanted to know how that would affect their position. Would they make or lose money? The company had excelled for them, having gained more than $3,000 since the original purchase and paid more than $200 in dividends. But the conversion was beyond their knowledge base, and they began to question whether they should continue to hold.

Elizabeth, who was reviewing the company, had heard some talk about a reduced dividend when the company became a corporation. Pierre lamented the company's introduction of a credit card, noting that it might represent too much expansion. Charlotte countered that the card business might be a worthwhile effort to diversify from its cleaning service businesses. Since the group's consensus was to hold, it moved on to other business concerning potential additions to the portfolio and how dividend reinvestment plans worked.

Questions that went unanswered got "tabled" for review at a later date. Requests for more information were delegated to a member or two. On the subject of dividend reinvestment plans, discussion focused on saving some money on brokerage fees, which was where DRPs could help. So Charlotte efficiently assigned Pierre and Binnie to investigate. Thus, having survived any major sell decisions that evening, the club kept up its regimen of research and monitoring. It also stuck closely to its agenda, which helped avert digressions that so often derailed meetings.

By no means is this section a suggestion to time your trades according to what you or some analyst says is happening in the market. This has proven to be a bad idea over time. Most people—even the pros—consistently guess wrong. But from time to time certain conditions crop up that may allow you to get a better price. Nevertheless, the following advice is probably best for moving a large position in or out of the market (in other words, if you need to cash out a large portion of your portfolio to pay for college or retirement expenses).

Your safest way of getting into the market over time is still dollar-cost averaging. Surprisingly, even if you buy into the market at every peak (followed by a decline), you'd still make money. For example, a study by the American Funds group found that $5,000 invested in the S&P 500 index peaks over a twenty-year period (1973–92) still would have generated $460,356. That's because despite the worst possible timing, the market always bounced back. There's no point in even trying to time the market. To beat a buy-and-hold approach, you'd need to "catch 80 percent of the market moves" to make money, Tom O'Hara notes.

## WHEN TIMING IS RIGHT

Due to the wonderful quirks of human nature, some days are better than others in terms of timing your trade. Research has shown that certain patterns hold true when it comes to prime days for buying and selling. The best known of these cycles is "the January effect," in which big run-ups are usually posted in the first month of winning years. Of course, these guidelines don't work 100 percent of the time but should serve as indicators of when to get the best possible price.

Although your analysis of the right price will largely determine this, certain days are swayed by large institutional trades. The end of quarters (March 31, June 30, September 30, and December 31) are when portfolio managers spruce up their portfolios for quarterly reports. The period just before holidays also tends to buoy prices, since traders are in a good mood and anxious to take off. Markets have climbed almost 72 percent in these periods over the past forty-two years. You can often get a good price on Mondays during the middle of the months of February, April, June, and October. These have been historical low points for stocks (especially Octobers). Maybe it's true that rainy days and Mondays always get Wall Street down.

The presidential cycle is another phenomenon that almost guarantees you a good price. Although there are hundreds of other theories on timing based on cycles and behavior—involving everything from astrology to chaos—one proven cycle is worth noting when timing purchases: the presidential "honeymoon" effect. Typically, the market will go up during the first week (often up to one year) of a president's term. Then, almost like clockwork, some crisis will emerge in the middle of the term, effectively ending the honeymoon, and the market will take a tumble. One exception was Richard Nixon's second term: following a honeymoon that lasted 3½ weeks, the nation suffered one of the worst bear markets in the last thirty years, dropping some 43 percent during 1973 and 1974.

When the headlines scream sell, however, that's when you should be sharpening your pencil and calling your broker. Here are some examples of market bottoms that offered prime buying opportunities:

### The Presidential Cycle: Buying Opportunities

| Year | President | Event/Notes |
| --- | --- | --- |
| 1958 | Eisenhower | Sputnik/Khrushchev/Cold War |
| 1962 | Kennedy | Bay of Pigs |
| 1966 | Johnson | Vietnam escalation |
| 1970 | Nixon | Civil unrest, Cambodia/Vietnam |
| 1974 | Nixon | Watergate, first Arab oil embargo |
| 1978 | Carter | Recession begins; Iranian revolt |
| 1982 | Reagan | Inflation (then Fed tightening) |
| 1986 | Reagan | S&L's, Iran/contra, crash in October 1987 |
| 1990 | Bush | Persian Gulf War |
| 1994 | Clinton | Interest rates rise, Whitewater |

Notice a pattern here? Every four years or so, some crisis precedes either a downturn or a bear market. Of course, there are other factors that may or may not have anything to do with what happens in the White House. A Federal Reserve hike in interest rates, for example, tends to put a damper on the stock and bond markets. The point is, had you bought nearly any stock during these gloomy periods—and held on—you would've made money.

There's a reason savvy investors from Joseph P. Kennedy to Warren Buffett bought while everybody else was selling: they knew they were getting a great price and that the market would eventually turn around. Consequently they made money.

What if you think you're stuck in a bear market? You have no idea how long these dour periods will last. Again, the advice is consistent with what you've always done when the market was robust. There have been thirty bear markets since 1900, about one every three years. They usually last only about a year and nudge the Dow Industrial Average down about 26 percent. Do you like the idea of getting 26 percent off quality merchandise? That's one way of looking at it.

As Ralph Acampora, director of technical analysis for Prudential Securities, told investment clubbers in Milwaukee, "If the market continues to 'correct,' keep your powder dry, do your research, and buy more [of the quality stocks you've selected]."

## The Best Time to Sell Stocks

Again, rely heavily upon your fundamental analysis before making this kind of decision. Historical high points have fallen on Fridays toward the end of trading hours in December, July, and August. These are the best days during a bull market. During a bear market, however, you probably won't have as many rosy opportunities to reap profits.

## Buying and Selling Mutual Funds

All open-end funds (see page 227) go *ex-dividend* either at the end of a quarter or in late December. That means they pay out dividends and capital gains (if they have them) on appointed days. When this occurs, the *net asset value* (NAV)—the average of all securities prices divided by the number of shares outstanding—drops by the per-share amount of the dividend. If you're buying, the best time is right after the ex-dividend date. If you're selling, the best time is right before this date. This way you avoid the additional taxation of the dividend (unless the fund's in an

IRA, which is not subject to tax). Call your mutual fund company's investor hotline for specific information about their ex-dividend dates.

Since they issue a fixed number of shares, *closed-end* mutual funds (see page 228) work like stocks. They are heavily promoted at the initial public offering to boost the share price. Once the promotional period is over—usually after six months or so—you'll get a better price. Ideally, you should buy a closed-end at a *discount* to net asset value (5 percent discount for stocks funds is reasonable; 4 percent for bond funds). A useful sell signal is when the fund hits a premium of 10 percent or more or lags funds of its objective by more than 5 percent.

## Buying and Selling Bonds

Of course, there's no need to go through a broker if you're buying U.S. Treasury securities. They are auctioned on a regular schedule to pay off Washington's ever-expanding debt. Better yet, you pay no commission if you buy directly through the government. The "Treasury Direct" program will even store the bonds for you and pay interest automatically (through electronic funds transfer to a bank account of your choosing). No muss, no fuss. For more information, contact the Federal Reserve at (804) 697-8355 or your nearest Federal Reserve Bank branch. The best time to buy bonds is when rates are high; the best time to sell is when rates start to rise. This reasoning applies to certificates of deposit as well. Bond prices drop when interest rates climb as investors scramble to unload lower-yielding securities for higher market rates. So if you don't hold a bond to its maturity, you may lose principal value. Generally, the shorter the maturity, the more stable the market price. Therefore, thirty-year bonds are the most volatile. A one-percentage point rise will send a thirty-year Treasury price down 10 percent. Similar zero-coupon bonds may fall as much as 30 percent under the same market move. If you're in money market funds, however, the portfolio manager will get you the highest short-term rates anyway without loss of principal.

Someone once asked the legendary multibillionaire investor Warren Buffett what was his average holding time for the stocks he bought. "Forever," is said to be his response. As a simple rule, if your stocks are performing to your expectations—and you don't need the money—hold on to them. There's no hard-and-fast rule about taking your profit after the price reaches a certain level. The best stocks keep climbing and splitting for decades on end. When it comes to market timing, even the most educated and experienced traders guess wrong. There are thousands of market timing methods and techniques that almost always fail most of the time.

The industry is filled with newsletter gurus announcing that they pulled investors out before a downturn or got them in just before a major upward move. Such self-congratulation is largely a marketing device. What these "experts" don't tell you about is all the other moves they just plain missed. If you read Mark Hulbert's column in *Forbes* or read his newsletter, you know that most market timers are wrong most of the time. Oh, they occasionally get lucky. But the opportunities they miss far outweigh their best guesses. To keep your perspective on market timing, remember what H. L. Mencken said when describing Wall Street: "It's a thoroughfare that begins in a graveyard and ends in a river."

Here are some useful guidelines that will help you determine when to sell a stock, although no one guideline should be used by itself. As with stock selection, weigh a number of factors before making a decision.

• *The company's management has faltered in a number of measurable ways*—sales have dropped off, productivity is down, products are lagging the competition. Your job is to gauge whether current management is slipping: Has the current management team kept up with industry, national, and global developments? Have they taken a bath on too many unprofitable product lines? Do they have any new products/services in the pipeline?

• *The company's fundamentals are unfavorable.* Price, price/earnings, and profits are down relative to the management factors. Has the company significantly boosted its debt-to-equity ratio? Again, keep running the numbers and see how the company stacks up against its competition. Is it lagging by more than 10 percent? Has it cut its dividend recently?

• *Global, governmental, or industry trends have left the company behind.* Is the company still selling yesterday's unprofitable technology? Is it stuck in a country where government interference prevents any reasonable growth? Is an industry shakeout leaving it in the dust?

• *You're emotionally committed to a stock.* This is usually a negative consideration. Make sure you don't let yourself lose sight of the aforementioned fundamentals. Don't hang on to a hamburger chain stock just because you like their burgers. You may be in an increasingly smaller group.

• *The stock in question is lagging and you have a stronger stock to replace it.*

## WHEN TO SELL

It doesn't hurt to look ahead when a company is doing well and it's an irresistible "hold." That especially applies to companies that have consistently been solid money-makers—even they still bear close scrutiny. The NAIC has portfolio review methods called "PERT" and "Challenge Trees" (explained in detail in the NAIC manual) that are used to test portfolio holdings on a continuing basis.

If you want to review a stock, review the fundamentals. Ask yourself (or your club members) the following:

1. Has there been a major news announcement indicating material changes in the company's financial picture?
2. Has a change in management negatively impacted the company's outlook for growth?
3. Has the market(s) in which the company operates changed to disfavor the company's product and marketing?
4. Are there similar stocks that offer more promising growth potential?
5. Is the stock just failing to meet your expectations?

## WHEN NOT TO SELL

Ralph Seger, who picks stocks for the NAIC's Investment Advisory Service, takes a disciplined approach when it comes to selling. The seventy-six-year-old money manager began his quest for investing knowledge out of concern for unfunded pension liabilities at Uniroyal Tire, where he worked as an engineer in the

1960s. When he couldn't get into the investment club at Uniroyal, he started his own.

In January 1979 he took early retirement and did volunteer work for the NAIC. By 1981 he felt confident enough to start his own investment counseling business and hung out his shingle with two clients. He's never lost money for his clients and now manages $30 million.

Despite the drubbing health care stocks have endured in 1993–94, Ralph has steadfastly recommended stocks like Abbott Labs and American Home Products. He's undeterred by the bad publicity because he takes a hard look at basic financial details.

Abbott Labs, for example, has run a gauntlet of lawsuits (by shareholders, competitors, and the government) in recent years. Its troubles have been compounded by the uncertainty over health care reform and the market's wariness of pharmaceuticals in general. Institutions dumped stocks like Abbott, Merck, and AHP en masse.

Most stocks keep rising after a split, reflecting eager investors buying more shares at lower prices. For Abbott, though, the bad news kept coming. At an NAIC council meeting, a company representative headed off questions on a $50 million shareholder price inflation lawsuit and a price-fixing suit concerning Abbott's marketing of infant formula. The company was even receiving flak from consumer groups opposed to a prescription "lollipop" that dispensed medicine to children.

Abbott, ninth in the NAIC top holdings list, was causing stockholders anguish. But at the core of the company's financials and management were some impressive numbers that kept on improving no matter what the stock market did. Here's a summary:

## Abbott Labs

15.3% compounded annual growth
Potential price gain of 59% to 123%
Earnings/share growth of 10%
P/E of 14.3 (considerably below the S&P 500 average)
Steady dividend growth
14.1% compounded growth for research and development (critical for a pharmaceutical firm)
Increasing sales/employee (productivity)
Growing market shares in all of its market segments

Source: Abbott Labs, NAIC Investor Advisory Service

Abbott's numbers indicate a robust uptrend. The lawsuits (some of which have been since settled) were deemed to be "nonmaterial"—that is, they wouldn't affect earnings. Does this illustration close the book on companies that generate more jitters than confidence? No. You always have to be vigilant by scanning the major business newspapers and magazines for news.

Ralph Seger uses a handful of screening measures to examine a possible sell candidate. Following are a few of his suggestions for gauging a possible sale:

- **Keep monitoring the stock for changes in earnings growth and management.**
- **Closely follow *earnings growth, pre-tax profit, earnings on equity capital, price/earnings ratio, and management.* Any change in these factors is important. "If management's bad, however, all of the other things don't matter."**
- **"If sales and earnings are no longer growing and you've lost faith in management, I would recommend a sale."**

- If a stock is hot and the market loves it, that may be a good time to bail out. "Trend investing will always bite you. If you can't find value, don't chase it." Many "momentum" investors get burned when the market turns against a once popular issue.

## THE BEAR MARKET

Clubs that started in the 1970s or in 1987 know this problem well: Suppose you're in a bad economy and the market is "bearish"? The best advice is to hang on and keep buying. The market will turn around and eventually reward you. As the following chart shows, bear markets have turned into bull markets in anywhere from three to sixty-four months. It all depends on your patience. So don't be cowed into thinking that everything is sour in the economy. For most long-term club members, a bear market is just an opportunity to buy quality companies at great prices.

Tom O'Hara, who's seen a few downturns with the NAIC over the past fifty years, recalls bear markets in 1965–66, 1970, and 1974–80, when stocks were about as popular as dentists working without anesthetics. These markets were so depressed that large institutions quit buying and there were typically more sellers than buyers. Consequently, NAIC club membership peaked in October 1970 and declined steadily for ten years. The one thousand members a week who had rushed into the NAIC during the 1960s diminished to a handful.

There was a lot of instability between Watergate, oil embargoes, and rampant inflation. Worse yet, if you had invested in the stock market, you were watching your portfolio lose value on a regular basis. Most investors have never seen a bear market com-

### Stock Market Declines of 15%+
### S&P 500—1953–93

| Year(s) | Decline % | Months | Months to Recover[*] 75% of Decline | 100% of Decline |
|---------|-----------|--------|-------------------------------------|-----------------|
| 1953    | 15%       | 9      | 4                                   | 6               |
| 1956–57 | 16        | 6      | 3                                   | 5               |
| 1957    | 20        | 3      | 11                                  | 12              |
| 1961–62 | 29        | 6      | 10                                  | 14              |
| 1966    | 22        | 9      | 5                                   | 6               |
| 1968–70 | 37        | 18     | 9                                   | 22              |
| 1973–74 | 48        | 21     | 20†                                 | 64              |
| 1975    | 15        | 2      | 2                                   | 4               |
| 1977–78 | 18        | 14     | 1                                   | 6               |
| 1978    | 17        | 2      | 7                                   | 10              |
| 1980    | 22        | 2      | 3                                   | 4               |
| 1981–82 | 22        | 13     | 2                                   | 3               |
| 1987    | 34        | 2      | 18                                  | 23              |
| 1990    | 20        | 3      | 5                                   | 5               |
| Average | 28%       | 8      | 7                                   | 13              |

[*] From market low
†50% of decline recovered in five months
Source: David L. Babson & Co.

parable to the one twenty years ago. In the middle of the 1970s, O'Hara's Mutual Club of Detroit saw its total portfolio plummet from $600,000 to $320,000. O'Hara said even his wife wanted him to pull out and spend the money. But he stayed in. Today that portfolio's worth more than $2.5 million.

"I told people across the country to just stick with it. Practically all of the clubs had losses. It's harder to invest in the market when it's going down. But I found that if a person goes through a down market and recovery, they've hooked [into stock market investing] for life."

The best strategy to ride out a bear market is to focus on quality. Those companies that are not cyclical plays or devastated by major economic moves will be even more focused in the event of major economic downturns. Bad times make good companies even better. The advice in this area is short and sweet: If the management and fundamentals of the company remain sound, stay the course. You have more to lose by abandoning ship.

If you're still bewildered by the possibility that the market may crash any time now, here are some sound strategies for avoiding "bear fever":

1. *Avoid the market altogether if the money you're investing will be needed within the next five years for other things.* Having personally drained most of my investment club portfolio to pay for kitchen cabinets, I can attest to the toxic effect short-term cash needs have upon a portfolio (especially when the stocks you sell have already been bombed by health care politics).
2. *If there is a downturn, remember that there's always an upturn.* The stock market's long-term curve is upward. The crash of 1987 looked like the end of the world to some but like huge buying opportunities to those who took advantage of them.

## THE BOTTOM LINE: QUALITY

As Peter Lynch has stated hundreds of times, "If you purchase the stock of a well-managed company and hold it for the long

haul (at least ten years), your investment is bound to appreciate."
Lynch notes that a good example is Coca-Cola: if you bought
Coke at thirty times earnings in the 1960s, your investment
would've increased thirty-two-*fold* by 1993. His observation is
echoed by billionaire investor Warren Buffett, who has had a
large stake in Coca-Cola for years and keeps buying more.

The Stock Barons, ever amused and amazed by the titans of
Wall Street, follow the words of Lynch and Buffett the way
groupies trail rock stars. The Barons are holding tight to their best
acquisition: AFLAC. It also doesn't hurt that Lynch recommends
it. Fretting over their positions in PepsiCo, Merck, McDonald's,

## Reduction of Risk over Time 1925–93

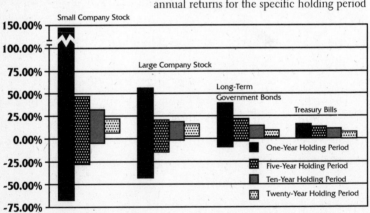

Each bar shows the range of compound average
annual returns for the specific holding period

Source: Ibbotson Associates

Safety-Kleen, and Wal-Mart, they carefully discuss the perceived direction of each company. In their own way, they are performing "quality reviews" of the companies. For now, they are waiting out the cycles that plague these companies.

In the meantime, they hope that some of the wisdom of Wall Street will rub off on them as they travel insightfully through *The Wall Street Journal* and *Value Line* surveys. Velma, in particular, "can't wait until I can buy my first share of [Buffett's company] Berkshire Hathaway." At $29,000 a share and no splits in sight (at this writing), it may be a long wait.

# CHAPTER 12

# Mutual Funds

Investfact: Even in 401(k) pension plans—where long-time employees can afford to take risks in tax-deferred mutual funds—a survey found that a meager 6 percent of those polled invested in stocks, according to Hewitt Associates. Less than 2 percent of employee funds went into aggressive growth or international stock funds, which have the best combined records over time.

Investment clubs typically don't bother with mutual funds because they pick their own stocks. There are situations, however, when your club should consider a fund for specialized forms of investing. International, small-cap, and technology stocks are notoriously difficult to follow and price. In these situations, a fund manager and a staff of researchers might help you and your club diversify.

Although most fund managers don't even beat the market, when you have a good one, it's like having the best research and stock pickers in the world on your side. There are now more than four thousand mutual funds. That's more than all the stocks on the New York Stock Exchange. Choosing one is often like picking a doctor out of the Yellow Pages. Once you get past all the specialists, chiropractors, and osteopaths, you realize that you don't have any idea how to find a practitioner who's right for you.

Mutual funds exist because drive-up windows on restaurants and banks exist. Most people just don't have the time to research hundreds of stocks and bonds, know when to buy and sell, and answer the phones when the market crashes. Even if you're willing to do most of that work anyway—except answer the phones—you still might need some mutual funds to round out your portfolio.

As investment pools that employ professional managers, funds fall into three camps: poor, average, and exceptional. Unfortunately, most rate the first two categories *because they don't do their research*. Assuming that you want a fund to give you a specialized play or more diversification, you need to find one that does take research seriously—just as you must, in determining which fund is right for you.

No matter how you feel about funds in general, you have to concede that some are better than others and many excel in specialties—like international and small-cap investing—where you don't have access to the resources they do. That's why it pays to add them to your portfolio to diversify and reduce risk.

This may sound surprising, but when your club invests in a fund, you lose investment control. The majority of mutual funds are *open-end*, meaning that every time new money comes in, new shares are created. Hotter performers, therefore, are constantly creating new shares and looking for places to invest the cash. That puts a strain on most fully invested stock funds. When the market turns south, the opposite is true. During the crash of 1987, hundreds of fund managers had to liquidate stock positions to meet redemptions. Despite what fund managements claim, there's no way they can remain "buy and hold" players when dire events occur.

*Closed-end* mutual funds, by contrast, issue a fixed number of shares and trade like a stock on exchanges. Closed-ends include everything from bond funds to single-country funds. You buy them through brokers and figure your performance based on market value and net asset value (NAV—the average of all securities prices divided by the number of shares outstanding). Open-end mutual funds figure performance based only on NAV. Unlike their open-end brethren, closed-end funds hold on to their positions as long as they like. Redemptions are made by trading shares on an exchange. Although there are only a handful of closed-end funds, they allow managers more freedom and specialization.

What do funds do that you can't do? Well, really nothing, except they can do it in volume and with greater efficiency. Every fund employs a staff of analysts who look for the best buys in specific areas. Say you need a fund that specializes in technology stocks because you (and your club members) are particularly uninformed or squeamish in that area. You know that certain technologies will be surging over the next decade, but you don't know the difference between a microprocessor and a food processor. So you're paying for the expertise.

Here are some of the specialized fund categories:

- *Aggressive Growth/Small Company.* The high-performance sports cars of funds, these stay invested in stocks all the time for maximum returns—and risk. They invest in everything from unproven small companies to earnings-driven blue chips. They are among the riskiest groups in the short term yet over decades easily beat all other categories (if well managed).

- *Growth.* These are stock funds that generally follow companies with consistent earnings, although they usually aren't as risky as growth funds.
- *Growth & Income/Equity-Income.* Conservative, yield-oriented stock funds that combine stocks with healthy dividends and occasionally bonds.
- *Balanced.* Combining a fixed percentage of stocks and bonds, these funds are for the most conservative equity investors.
- *Income.* Bonds of every stripe occupy this niche, from U.S. government obligations to risky corporate "junk" (high-yield) bonds.
- *Overseas, Global, and Foreign.* Also called "emerging markets" funds, these foreign securities vehicles get as specialized as one region (Asia or Europe, for example) or cover the entire world.
- *Sector.* The most specialized of fund groups, they cover single industries (autos, food) or subindustries (biotechnology, software). These are typically subsets of the aggressive growth or small-company funds.
- *Money Markets.* These are classic "parking places" for cash that emphasize short-term securities at an unchanging $1 per share NAV. No capital gains are possible from investing in these funds, so they are relatively safe.

## CHOOSING A FUND MANAGER

Once you or your club decides that a fund category addresses your diversification needs, it's time to get out your investment hoe and clear the weeds. The unusual thing here is that bad funds, unlike restaurants that serve bad food and go out of business, often manage to hang around for years, blithely attracting unwary investors.

Ideally, the fund(s) you choose should offer consistently above average returns relative to the risk they're taking. How do you measure this elusive factor? My best suggestion is to consult Morningstar Mutual Funds or magazines that feature their ratings. Morningstar uses a "star" rating system that measures a risk/return ratio. Their highest rating, five stars, means that the fund performed the best among its group with the least possible amount of risk. To date, theirs is one of the best measures of fund performance, although it is not a guarantee of future performance. Some funds have great years for a variety of reasons (perhaps because every stock fund did well that year, as was the case in 1993).

I recommend a risk/return rating over pure performance, primarily because it forces you to take a holistic look at the fund you're considering. Holistic evaluation involves a process similar to selecting single stocks, only there are more factors to consider. Among them:

- *Performance Periods.* Never trust a one-year performance record. The longer the period you have to study, the better. Unfortunately, most funds don't have twenty-year-plus records. So you have to settle for three-, five-, and ten-year records. "Total return" is the most relevant performance figure because it shows capital gains/losses minus fund expenses such as loads.
- *Yield.* If you're seeking income, this is one figure that's important.
- *Loads and Expenses.* You're better off not paying any load and the lowest possible expense ratio. Loads are commissions that fund groups exact from your money to pay brokers

and salespeople. There are thousands of no-load funds, and these should be your first preference. The expense ratio includes commissions and management fees. Usually, the larger the fund, the lower the expense ratio. Stock funds charging more than 1.50 percent a year for expenses are too expensive. Bond funds should charge half of that. Money market funds often waive their management fees.

- *12b-1 charges.* This is also called a "distribution" charge and ranges from .25 percent to 1.25 percent of the amount invested annually. These fees, imposed every year, often amount to greater burdens than onetime loads for long-term investors. Avoid funds that charge them. Again, your money's nicked to pay for the fund's marketing expenses.

- *Objective.* Although this is often a fuzzy term, it describes how the manager seeks to invest the fund. Some funds target stocks in the health care industry and ignore everything else. Other funds aim for growth from countries in the Asian Pacific region. The objective is one of the most closely monitored sections of a portfolio. Look for a fund whose objectives match yours.

- *Performance Relative to Objective.* This is a key screen that allows you to compare the fund's return relative to similar funds, an "apples to apples" comparison that gives you a better picture of how the fund did among its peers. Morningstar further measures this number in its "Morningstar risk" figure.

- *Cash Holdings.* The percentage of cash holdings isn't too revealing but tells you how much of the fund's money is invested in the market. Fully invested funds often are 10 percent to 20 percent invested in cash. Pessimistic fund managers, however, retreat to cash when they think the market is due for a downturn. They are, in effect, timing the market, which inspires more wrong guesses than anything else.

- *Sector Weightings.* These are percentage allocations in specific industry sectors, another key factor that will determine if you need the fund's expertise. Subgroups include natural resources (oil and gas, paper), industrial products (machine tools, equipment), consumer durables (vehicles, appliances), nondurables (food, beverages), retail trade, services, utilities, transportation, finance (banks, insurance), and multi-industry.

- *Fundamental Analysis.* If you really want to get specific and read a manager's mind, you can obtain information on average price/earnings, price/book, and earnings/growth rates.

- *Style Ratings.* What kind of investor is the manager? Does management favor growth (earnings), or value (low asset prices)? Small-, medium-, or large-capitalization companies or a blend? Morningstar will give a breakdown of all of the above.

- *Bond Ratings.* These factors include averaged weighted maturities, credit quality, duration, weighted prices, and coupons. Essentially, most of these figures tell you how risky the bond portfolio is relative to credit quality and maturity.

- *Turnover Ratio.* This percentage tells you how much of the portfolio is sold off each year. High-turnover funds generate higher expenses that can lower your returns if performance doesn't outweigh the increased trading costs.

- *Portfolio Manager.* While there are some stars in the business, they rarely do well every year and can't do well without a good fund family of analysts behind them. Good managers and families can make new, no-record funds exciting possibilities. You should also note if a fund has changed managers recently. In most cases, the best fund families have talented managers-in-waiting to take over hot-performing funds. Fidelity, Merrill Lynch, T. Rowe Price, and Invesco are good examples.

- *Market Price and Premium/Discount.* For closed-ends only, this indicates the price at which a fund was purchased or sold on an exchange and the difference between the fund's NAV and market price. A positive number indicates a premium; negative is a discount. While it's generally best to buy at a discount, good funds are all too often bought at premiums.
- *Alpha and Beta.* The alpha is the difference between a fund's actual performance and its expected performance, given its level of risk (measured by beta). A negative alpha denotes underperformance. Beta shows how much risk is taken on given the S&P 500's annual performance. A beta of 1.00 equals the market performance. Above 1.00 denotes more risk, below 1.00 denotes less. For example, a beta of 1.10 means the fund should beat the market by 10 percent in bull markets and drop (at least) 10 percent in down markets.

## WHAT FUND MANAGERS CANNOT DO

They can't read your mind, for one thing. If you're targeting a specific sector or industry and can't find the right allocation in a single fund, build the portfolio yourself. Remember, your portfolio is your own mutual fund, where you control the management expenses, stock allocation, and buy/sell decisions.

Fund managers make bad decisions just like anybody else. Although they are highly paid professionals, they guess and prognosticate. Some are right in a big way, while others flop. For example, Donald Yachtman was named Morningstar's "Fund Manager of the Year" in 1992, when he was with Selected Amer-

ican Shares. His fund had a stellar performance and risk/return
ratio up to that time. But the following year he left the company
to start his own fund—the Yachtman. In 1993 the same star manager did dismally. In 1994, the fund turned around smartly.

Nothing's guaranteed. We all have good years and bad. Peter
Lynch, one of the greatest managers of all time, had some of his
best years in the first half of his tenure at the Fidelity Magellan
fund. Then he quit, only to be replaced by a young manager who
lasted only a year. His second successor, Jeff Vinik, has done fairly well, however. So you have no control over who manages a
fund or for how long.

When he was at the helm of the T. Rowe Price Science and
Technology fund, Roger McNamee was one of the best technology fund managers in the business. Then he moved on to start a
venture capital business. His successor, though, supported by a
talented staff of analysts, has kept the fund among the top performers in its objective. So what you're looking for is a consistency in that specialty. The former will be guaranteed by the fund's
stated objective. The latter takes some searching. Although fund
groups spend millions in promotion and research, they can't
always produce the best managers. But if they provide a good
foundation, that at least ensures a measure of consistency that's
not tied to a manager. The best fund groups can do this.

An open-end fund manager—most notably in the sector fund
arena—is also hamstrung by fickle waves of investors riding a
trend. The Fidelity Telecommunications fund is a good case in
point. Nearly 80 percent of the new investors in that fund got in
just before it peaked. They promptly bailed out when some market
ghost spooked them into selling around Thanksgiving of 1993. No
manager in the world could have predicted that and prevented the

outflow of cash and position liquidations. Any manager faced with that prospect can throw his long-term strategies out the window.

Closed-end funds have less of a problem with huge investor swings but lose out when the general market sinks the price without warning. These funds, although diversified and professionally managed, trade like individual stocks and may be more volatile. If the market wants to dump on Asian closed-end funds and you are maintaining a portfolio position in one, you go down, too, even if your particular fund is conservative.

Fund managers also can't be expected to hold sway over a country's political or economic situation. The very reason so many Latin American and Asian markets have boomed in recent years is that governments there suppressed inflation and encouraged growth and free-market reforms. Chile, if you'll recall, was controlled by a military dictatorship for most of the last twenty years. Then the political situation changed, and it became one of the hottest stock markets in the world.

China is another great example. Although the majority of investors can't invest directly in the People's Republic of China, they can indirectly through the Hong Kong market. But in 1997, when Hong Kong reverts to the People's Republic, all bets may be off. Fund managers can't control what's going to happen, but they have a better insight into the possibilities because they maintain offices or researchers in the countries in which they invest.

There are ways to invest in foreign growth without venturing into mutual funds. Most large manufacturing and consumer goods concerns are multinationals selling into those markets. Coca-Cola and Motorola, for example, do nearly 40 percent of their business overseas. Because specialized funds are not immune to the politics and economies of foreign countries, they also add a sizable risk component to your portfolio. That risk can be reduced by finding domestic corporations with high overseas exposure.

On the other hand, a portfolio of foreign stocks reduces your risk to domestic markets. It works both ways. One thing's clear, though. It's better to have more diversification by stock category (overseas vs. domestic) than to have all of your holdings in the United States.

## HOW TO SCREEN THE RIGHT FUNDS FOR YOUR PORTFOLIO

This is a systematic process, like assembling a model from a kit. Walk through these steps when deciding on the right fund.

1. *Select Your Objective.* If you know the objective or category of the fund you need, start with that. Most fund rating services list funds by category, although every service is slightly different. Ask yourself, "What do I want the fund to do?" Do you want a fund that's invested solely in South America? Do you want a fund that focuses on information technology stocks? Pick an objective or two and examine a handful of fund prospectuses (by calling the toll-free fund hot lines).

2. *Performance and Risk Rating.* How did the fund do in up and down markets? How did it fare against funds of similar objectives? How often did it beat the S&P 500 (or Lehman Brothers index, if a bond fund)? What is the annual average return for the longest period of time recorded? Was it more or less risk averse?

3. *How Much Does the Fund Cost?* Does it have an undesirable front-end, back-end, reinvestment, or 12b-1 fee? Does it have an unusually high expense or turnover ratio? Does it have a

high cost of entry? Most funds take minimum investments of $1,000, but some are as high as $100,000.

4. *Consistency of Management.* How often has the fund changed managers? How long has the present manager been there? Have new managers changed objectives? This is what you're paying extra money for, because managers should have the expertise and longevity to be able to spot stocks and trends and profit from them over time.

## EMULATING GREAT FUND MANAGERS

If you're going to model your stock picking after somebody, you might as well pick the best. If you wanted to become a great baseball hitter, whom would you choose to emulate? Michael Jordan or Frank Thomas? The same applies to mutual fund investing. Find the managers who do well year after year while tempering risk. According to Investment Data, a New York–based investment research firm, the three most admired fund managers were Ralph Wanger, Warren Buffett, and Charles Royce, who (like Wanger) specializes in small-cap stocks and has an excellent record over the decades. Also on the list were Peter Lynch (retired), Jeff Vinik—Lynch's successor at Fidelity's Magellan fund—and James Stowers, who manages as part of a team at Twentieth Century Investments.

To gain insight into how these managers operate, order annual reports of their funds or hear them speak at Morningstar conferences (tapes are available). Their craftsmanship also shows up in the many analyses written about their funds.

Millions of words are written every day on mutual funds. They're listed in every major newspaper business section and examined by every business and personal finance magazine. In the final analysis, though, it comes down to what the ideal stock investor should do: invest for the long term in quality growth (or value) stocks. If you find funds that do well in this regard year after year, hold on to them.

## FUND GROUP SPECIALTIES

Each fund group has specialties that may not be available to most amateur investors. Following are some groups that have excelled in particular areas.

Calvert: socially responsible growth and income (800-368-2748)
Evergreen: small-company growth and income (800-235-0064)
Fidelity: industry sector funds and every other objective (800-544-8888)
Invesco: overseas, sector funds (800-525-8085)
Merrill Lynch: overseas/Pacific Basin (800-637-3863)
Neuberger & Berman: growth, income (800-877-9700)
Phoenix: growth and income, income (800-243-4361)
Royce group: small-company value funds (800-221-4268)
Scudder: income, overseas (800-225-2470)
T. Rowe Price: overseas, technology (800-638-5660)
Templeton (Franklin): overseas emerging markets (800-292-9293)
Twentieth Century/Benham: aggressive small company/bonds (800-345-2021)
Vanguard: low-cost sector and overseas (800-662-7447)

## FUND EXPENSES

No fund is free. You pay for management, administration, brokerage fees, and even marketing the fund to other people ("distribution"). You don't have to pay too much, though. Some of the best funds also have low expenses, which means your returns get boosted through their efficiencies of scale. Can you run your own mutual fund for less? Probably. But you can't match some fund groups' research abilities across global markets.

There's always a great debate over which is better, no-load or load funds. The answer to this question depends largely on the two funds being compared and how they perform relative to the risks they take. Generally, you don't want to pay additional fees like 12b-1's if you can avoid it.

## FUND RESOURCES

*Note: Some of these newsletters and handbooks should be in your public library. For a more detailed description of services, turn to page 262.*

**CDA/Weisenberger**, 1355 Piccard Dr., Rockville, MD 20850

*Donoghue's Moneyletter*, 290 Eliot St., Ashland, MA 01721

*Getting Started in Mutual Funds*, by Alan Lavine (John Wiley, 1994)

**Morningstar Mutual Funds**, *Morningstar Investor*, 225 W. Wacker Dr., Chicago, IL 60606; (800) 876-5005

*The Mutual Fund Encyclopedia, The Mutual Fund Letter*, 680 N. Lake Shore Drive, Chicago, IL 60611

*Mutual Fund Investing*, 7811 Montrose Rd., Potomac, MD 20854

*No-Load Fund Investor & Encyclopedia*, P.O. Box 318, Irvington-on-Hudson, NY 10533

# EPILOGUE

# Before You Invest, You Have to Save

Okay, you have mouths to feed and bills to pay. By the end of the month you're scratching your head and looking for another paycheck to arrive. Nobody said it was going to be easy transforming yourself and your family from consumer/spenders into saver/investors. But before you can even contemplate investing, you have to save and control your spending.

According to *The Wall Street Journal*, some 70 percent of adult Americans have nothing left after paying the bills. That's another great argument for paying yourself *before* you pay your bills. In an age of 401(k)s, Social Security, and IRAs, you'd think it would all be set up for us when we turned twenty-one. It isn't.

There are really only a few basic principles you need to know about investing, and I was convinced I knew every one of them in my sleep. But money is such an abstract and elusive concept. It's like a subatomic particle. Only when you study money's effect on everything around it can you truly define it. So I had a problem.

For me, investment clubs defined what money is through the people who joined the clubs. They all had one objective: Invest wisely for the future. Now this took some concentration, some-thing most of us aren't accustomed to doing. We'd like a brochure or video to explain it all in about four minutes. Then we write the check, without a hint of additional research. Invest-ment clubs don't work like that. They reach decisions after thor-ough research, using proven methods. Then they vote on what investments to buy. This takes time.

So you don't have the time or the inclination? Well, you can make time. But, as Goethe once wrote, "Whatever you can do, or dream you can, begin it. Boldness has genius, power and magic in it." The literary giant of German romanticism, however, didn't provide us with tips on how to get started investing, so here it goes.

## GET ORGANIZED

• *Write down your money goals and post it on your refrigerator door.* This seems to be an oft used and central location in most homes, so nobody can miss your savings manifesto. Your goals can be anything from early retirement to a vacation home. The beauty of this list is that you see it and can't help but read it every time you're hungry. If you see it at least three times a day for a year, that's 1,095 reinforcement messages a year! At this rate you might receive more positive savings signals than advertisements.

• *Save whatever you can, no matter how little.* The whole investment club movement was founded on a credo that $10 a month is a great start to prosperity. How do you jump-start your savings? *Pay yourself first* before you pay any bills. That is, put some money aside before you look at the rent/mortgage, credit card statements, and other little demons that need to be fed by your checkbook.

• *If you can't rely on paying yourself first, do it automatically.* Nearly every bank, credit union, money market account, company payroll, and brokerage account offers an automatic withdrawal service. That means you can automatically move funds into a savings/investment account without ever having to touch them. Company pension plans use this system. If you can't touch it, you can't spend it—or anguish over not having saved it.

• *Nuke your credit cards.* Pay them off every month to avoid finance charges. If you're running a balance, pay down the principal to zero. Credit cards are the worst imaginable way of using credit since finance charges average around 18 percent. Since there's no tax deduction for personal interest, that's money you'll never see again. The typical American household carries some $8,570 of nonmortgage debt. Moreover, we spend 23 percent more on purchases when we use plastic, according to the *People's Almanac*. If you own a credit card, make sure yours is a no fee and low interest. Dump any department store or gasoline cards. Never use them for cash advances. If you just save the amount you pay on credit card interest, you're well on your way.

• *Refinance your mortgage* (if current rates are at least two points below your mortgage rates and you plan to stay in your home for at least three years).

• *Save together.* Remember that cute little slogan from the mid-1970s, "Shower together, save water"? Well, saving is best reinforced by someone you care about. Significant others such as spouses, children, grandparents, and neighbors make saving a group effort. There's also an element of peer pressure. Nobody likes to renege on group savings goals. Just make savings a togetherness issue and you'll be on to investment clubbing in no time.

• *Know how much you're spending and how much you're worth.* This is a really simple process that'll tell you more about yourself and your household than anything else. The first item is to collect all your monthly bills and add them up. These — mortgage/rent, taxes, insurance, food, entertainment, dry cleaning, etc. — are your expenses. Collect them all and arrive at "Total Monthly Expenses." Then total up your after-tax or take-home pay and any other sources of income. This is your income side. Subtract expenses from your income and you'll either have a surplus or a deficit. If you want a much bigger picture, figure out your net worth by subtracting your liabilities (mortgage debt, credit cards, taxes, loans) from your assets (savings, pension funds, savings bonds). How much are you worth? Are you paying out more than you're taking in on a monthly basis? This is the foundation for your savings and investment plan. If you can save something every month from your income, then you're ready to join the wide world of investment clubbing.

• *The best "no-brainer" is saving a dollar a day and all of your pocket change,* suggests the National Center for Financial Education (NCFE). This could add up to $50 a month or more. This is what many investment clubbers start out with when they pool their investment funds.

• *Grocery shopping is usually a big ticket expense (over time).* The NCFE estimates that thirty cents on every take-home dollar is spent on food and household items. Many people simply overbuy. Always shop with a list — and never on an empty stomach. You'll do even better if you shop with coupons — and without kids and spouses. If you waste 15 percent every week on a $100 grocery bill, that's $780 a year.

• *Remember that the bigger-ticket items such as houses, cars, and appliances are always price-negotiable.* Best available prices for cars and appliances can be provided either by *Consumers Digest* or *Consumers Reports* magazines.

• *There are many ways to save on your home.* Check your property tax bill to see that it's in line with what your neighbors (who own similar properties) are paying. If not, contact your local taxing authority and file an appeal. Make sure that you have well-maintained, energy-efficient heating/cooling appliances. Make sure your house is properly insulated. Install energy-efficient windows if your windows leak air. Remember, energy lost from a poorly insulated house is your money flowing out into the ozone. Save money on heating/cooling, and you're investing in your future.

• *Last, but not least, there's the "petty cash" technique.* My wife, Kathleen, devised this little idea on how to rebuild our savings and cut down on ATM addiction and unneeded purchases. First she figured out what we *should* go through each week in out-of-pocket expenses. Then she took the money out of the bank and put it into a tea can. We were allowed to take money, but only if we accounted for each purchase to one another. Of course, we weren't to exceed the weekly "deposit." Other "regular" bills were to be paid for by check (except for gas, which we charged). The method has worked wonderfully and forced us to pack lunches and not raid the ATM every other day. It has also brought us closer together, because it's a joint project.

Looking for an extra $20 a month? Here are some more painless suggestions:

1. Buy items you need frequently in bulk at warehouse stores or co-ops.
2. If you qualify for a discount as a senior citizen or student, ask for it.

3. Bring your lunch to work.
4. Make your long-distance calls on weekend nights.
5. Either carpool or take public transportation.
6. Pay cash for items where a cash discount is offered.
7. Fix your own meals at home from scratch instead of going out or buying prepared foods.
8. Do some of your own car maintenance such as oil changes and battery and fluid replacement.
9. Wait for seasonal sales, such as Christmas decorations in January or landscaping plants in October.
10. Bargain for everything that doesn't have a fixed price. Some excellent values can be obtained this way.

## INDIVIDUAL INVESTING

Most club investors find that their club experiences have been essential in guiding their own portfolio strategies. But there are some things you can do on your own that you can't really do in a club:

1. Write down your financial goals (retirement, college, second home, and so on). Update them every year and check to see that you are meeting them.
2. Make sure that your insurance needs are covered. If you have dependents, you'll need life insurance for the bread-winner(s). Don't buy life insurance unless you have children or others to support. If you're working, make sure you're covered by a good disability policy. You're far more likely to become disabled—and lose income—than die unexpectedly.
3. Without hesitating, fully fund all of your company and per-

sonal retirement vehicles. These include 401(k)s, 403(b)'s, IRAs, SEP-IRAs, and Keoghs. These are, by far, the best tax breaks you'll ever get. Fund them to the max!

4. Know how much money you need to "keep liquid" for short-term expenses such as emergencies or things such as car or appliance purchases. Keep this money in "cash"—safe money market or short-term bond funds. These funds won't make you rich, but they'll be there when you need it. If you have to dip into your long-term investments for short-term money, you're not planning carefully enough.

5. Invest on your own every opportunity you get. Why wait?

Now's the time to apply all of the knowledge gained from investment clubbing. Again, not every stock you pick will be a winner. Nor should you expect to see *immediate* results. There's risk in everything, but it can be mitigated using a low-impact, long-term approach. Would you bet all of your mortgage money on a single stock? Nevertheless, you have the leeway in your own portfolio to expand positions in your club's portfolio or to choose stocks that go beyond the club's resources.

Just keep in mind that you're aiming for results that beat inflation and accumulate and compound over time. Time is on your side if you go slowly.

## MY PORTFOLIO AND
## WHAT YOU CAN LEARN FROM IT

Like a lot of people, I have to try it to see if it's any good. To test the rigors of investment clubbing, I joined the National Association of Investment Clubs. I wanted to see firsthand if my wife, Kathleen, and I could build a portfolio and make money.

I've had some success in picking mutual funds and some small purchases in stocks. I should've done well. I've had access to some of the best information on investing in the world over the past ten years, with subscriptions to *Barron's*, *The Wall Street Journal*, *The New York Times*, *Money*, *Kiplinger's Changing Times*, *Worth*, *Smart Money*, *Business Week*, *Forbes*, *Morningstar Mutual Funds*, and hundreds of other newsletters. Not only did I read every issue of these publications during the last decade, I freelanced for *Barron's* and knew the gentlemen who started Morningstar. I also attended every biannual Morningstar conference, heard and interviewed the most brilliant mutual fund managers of all time (from Peter Lynch to Ralph Wanger), and attended one major investing conference per year.

And I made money selecting mutual funds. Then Kathleen thought we should pick stocks. She knew of a growing network software company called Novell that she believed would make a good buy. We bought at $13 and sold at $28, nervously locking in our profits. Later Novell went to $65. Buying one-hundred-share lots, we were big rollers. Although I had made some money buying Continental Bank and International Harvester (now Navistar) at distressed prices, I never really saw myself as a speculative investor. I always bought quality companies in bad situations that turned around, never on margin or through a large position. I was guaranteeing myself never to take a loss or get too rich from this thing. And I never invested more than $1,000 at a time in any one stock.

In the late 1980s we poured most of our money into mutual funds. I played around with some aggressive growth and gold mutual funds during up cycles and exchanged out of them during downturns. Before we were married, I even speculated on platinum and palladium bullion. I made enough money on the platinum to buy Kathleen a one-carat diamond engagement ring. I bought the palladium on a hunch that automakers would use the metal in catalytic converters instead of platinum because it was substantially cheaper. Years later it turned out I was right, but I lost money on that investment because I needed the money for something else and sold at a loss, which is a consistent investment strategy killer.

The mutual funds I picked nearly all did well. I picked the best funds with the proven managers. I would stay in a year or so, take a profit, and move on. During the crash of 1987, we pretty much stayed in funds (with one exception) and witnessed a healthy rebound. It was a scary time, but we didn't lose money because we stayed the course.

One fund I stayed in three years — the Invesco Strategic Health Sciences Portfolio — rose 120 percent during the time we held it. Health care stocks were the rage of Wall Street during the late 1980s. But in 1991, as it became plausible that Bill Clinton would win the presidency and reform U.S. health care, these stocks took a dive. I got out but still doubled the money in Kathleen's IRA. Our other IRAs weren't doing as well, but they were averaging from 15 percent to 30 percent a year. So I felt we were making the right choices there with little pain.

In 1991 Kathleen decided she wanted to start her own software business. Since she was a top salesperson with every company she had worked for, we figured this was a good bet. Unfortunately, no banks would accept mutual funds in IRAs as collateral. Only stocks, bonds, certificates of deposit, and cash were considered. So out of necessity I built a $10,000 portfolio of twenty-one individual stocks. After several months' research and joining the

NAIC, I started to buy through a discount broker. It helped somewhat that a recession was on and there were some bargains out there.

My initial strategy was to diversify with a mixture of big pharmaceuticals and utilities (their dividends were generous), food companies (generally recession proof), environmental services (they were battered but due for rebounds), and technology. Here's what the portfolio looked like (NAIC-recommended or low-cost investment program stocks are footnoted):

| **Stock** | **Bought** | **Sold** |
|---|---|---|
| Abbott Labs | 28 | 27½ |
| Allied Waste* | 4¼ | 5½ |
| Archer Daniels-Midland | 29½ | 26⅝ |
| Autodesk | 30 | 50 |
| Bristol-Myers Squibb | 80 | 55⅝ |
| Citizens Utilities† | 37⅕ | 30¾ |
| ConAgra | 30 | 26⅝ |
| Frame Technologies | 23¼ | 9 |
| Heinz | 29 | 36½ |
| Eli Lilly | 71 | 55½ |
| Motorola | 40 | Still holding/3 splits |
| NYNEX | 70¾ | 93 |
| Quaker Oats | 55 | 64 |
| RPM‡ | 21⅞ | 18⅞ |
| Royce Value Trust | 11 | Still holding |
| Rubbermaid | 31½ | 34⅜ |
| Safety-Kleen | 22 | 17 |
| TECO Energy | 37⅜ | 42¾ |
| U.S. West | 38 | 47 |

| Stock | Bought | Sold |
|-------|--------|------|
| Walgreen's | 36 | 40⅝ |
| Western Waste | 14¼ | 19¾ |
| Unit | 1¼ | 2½ |

Notes: * = posted 1 for 2 reverse split in 1993; † = split 2 for 1 in 1993; ‡ = split 2 for 1 in 1993. Share prices do not represent average DRP purchase prices.

Within one month of purchase, every stock I bought (save for two) had risen. I felt like a genius. I was "beating the street." I bragged to Kathleen. Then she told me she didn't really need the loan for her business. At this point I assumed that ours would be a long-term portfolio that would test my wits and allow me to compare my performance with the top-ranking mutual funds I had chosen for our IRAs. I was up to the challenge.

The first few months of the portfolio only fueled my investment bravura. Citizens Utilities split two for one. Autodesk zoomed from 30 to 50 and bounced around a lot. Motorola split *thrice*. Wherever possible, I enrolled in a stock company's dividend reinvestment plan, so I was buying new shares and reinvesting dividends commission free. With top-quality stocks like Bristol-Myers Squibb paying out a 5 percent dividend, I felt real smart. Then, as the fall turned to winter, reality hit.

Bad PR about the pharmaceutical industry caused an avalanche in the drug stocks. Although I thought I had bought at distressed prices, I didn't know from distress until after Mrs. Clinton started bemoaning "excessive profits" in the industry. Bristol-Myers Squibb, which I'd bought at 80, plummeted to 55⅜. Lilly nosedived from 71⅛ to 55½. Abbott split from 60 to 30, then dropped to 25. At first I was taken aback. I had believed I was already buying at the low point of these stocks. How dare the market abuse them further!

Figuring that the drug stocks had spilled enough blood, IVs, pills and whatever else they made, I bought at even lower prices through my dividend reinvestment plans (DRPs). This not only lowered my average cost, but bought me more shares without paying commissions.

Then disaster struck. After tapping out our free cash, a home equity loan, and additional income, we needed money for some badly needed home repairs and renovations. Although we hadn't bought our home as an investment, it was becoming a chasm of despair and a rather efficient black hole into which money disappeared. The house would not only eat most of our cash for three years, it would devour our stock portfolio, which was fast resembling certain sections of the rotting house. After several hair-pulling sessions, we decided to liquidate most of the stock portfolio.

Of course, having joined the NAIC and accepted their basic investing principles, I was going to violate one of their prime directives. It was like being on *Star Trek* and interfering with an alien culture. My long-term portfolio was becoming a short-term one. Hopeful positions were going to translate into capital losses. I also discovered that it was too big anyway, at least for only $10,000. Half a dozen stocks would've done the trick easily; twenty-two was spreading it a bit too thin. I knew my dream of beating the street was over when Bristol-Myers Squibb decided to limit its DRP to one hundred shares or more to eliminate pesky investors like me. I received my seventeen pathetic shares in the mail shortly after January 1, 1994. Over a three-month period I sold most of my small positions, reaping small losses. It was not a happy time.

My twelve winning positions were ravaged by broker's commissions and the fact that they'd been small purchases all along; so they represented either paltry gains or net losses. My seven losers were my best hopes for the future. You'll note I haven't calculated percentage gains or losses. I'd like *you* to look up current stock prices and figure my net. It'll be interesting to see what's turned around and what headed south. Was I right about the drug stocks?

Having been chastened by this experience, I resolved to concentrate on a few long-term positions that I would hold for years. Take heart, though: there's a happy ending. During the final phases of this book, I related some of the success stories to my wife. That inspired her not only to overhaul our family spending, but also to start an investment club for our family. The better part of this story is that the few stocks we held are making money and Kathleen and I are rebuilding the portfolio as members of our family investment club. We're in it for the long haul, knowing that even though there will inevitably be downturns along the way, the stock market always rises—and so will our investments.

# Investor's Magna Charta

George Nicholson, one of the founders of the NAIC, has been active in promoting investor rights for more than forty years. Since Nicholson developed and embellished most of the NAIC's core strategies, most NAIC stalwarts point to him as the soul of the investment club movement. According to Nicholson, individual investing is a worldwide movement that entitles investors to a certain set of guiding principles.

Nicholson's "Investor's Magna Charta," adopted in 1980 by the World Congress of Investment Clubs, is an interesting statement of principles that should be referred to when dealing with brokers and companies. The Magna Charta outlines some important ideals to remember as an investor. Not only are you contributing to your own wealth, you're creating jobs, keeping the world economy buoyant, and improving standards of living. So in effect you are more than just a citizen of a particular country. This document invokes Adam Smith, Thomas Jefferson, and Milton Friedman.

The main thrust of these guidelines is to remind you of your rights as an investor. There are also laws protecting your rights, but in order to enjoy these rights, you have to be informed and active in upholding and expanding them. Whether you work through your own investment club or contact shareholder relations departments directly, it's essential to make yourself heard.

## PRINCIPLES

1. Our social structure is based on a cooperation between capital and labor; therefore rights of private ownership and labor should be guaranteed.

2. Producing freely by individually owned enterprises on behalf of a free market implies carrying risks. The risk-bearing capital of the enterprise is an indispensable factor to progress, just as labor, creativity, inventiveness, and social attitude. The possibility of participating in the risk-bearing capital of the enterprise should be optimally guaranteed, avoiding any discrimination between the different categories of shareholders.

3. Personal share ownership should be stimulated by means of information and education. The consideration is that as many people as possible should be both risk-bearing and profit-sharing within the given social structure and organization of the society. The rights of an investor as an individual who invests his/her money directly or indirectly in securities should be safeguarded.

4. Public authorities should aim at such policy that besides payment of interest, a fair compensation for the risk involved can be required from share-capital, by means of a true association of shareholders to the management in creating a real shareholders constituency.

5. Freedom of international transfer of capital should be promoted. Discrimination against foreign investors should be avoided.

6. As far as the Stock Exchange authorities are concerned, investors' confidence should be encouraged by adequate publicity concerning transactions and companies.

7. In Summary: Investment in securities as a form of wealth should be promoted by the government through legal measures, since through the acquisition of securities citizens will be able to participate even with a small capital input in the profit and growth of a business and thereby in the progress of the nation, further in the building of an enlightened world economy.

# GLOSSARY

**After-Tax Profit Margin.** The company's net income divided by revenues. "Pre-tax" is the same ratio before income taxes are subtracted.

**American Depository Receipts.** These are certificates that represent shares of foreign companies on American exchanges. Share prices are in dollars.

**Analysts.** A group of professionals responsible for evaluating companies and their future prospects for financial growth. Typically credentialed as certified financial analysts, they usually work for large brokerage houses, institutions, and investment advisers.

**Arbitration.** A system of resolving conflicts out of court. If you need to resolve a dispute with a licensed NASD securities broker, call (212) 480-4881 for their arbitration kit.

**Average Daily Trading Volume.** Also expressed simply as "volume" in stock listings, the ADTV reflects average volume in number of shares traded averaged over a year.

**Beta.** A statistical measure of risk that compares a stock's price performance (including dividends) with the overall fluctuation of the Standard & Poor's 500 index. If a stock has a beta of 1.00, it equals the S&P 500 in variance. If it's less than one, it's less risky than the index, vice versa for betas exceeding 1.00.

**Blue Chip.** A general reference to a large, established company that pays out consistent dividends and improves earnings on a regular basis.

**Capital Expenditures (as percentage of cash flow).** How much money is spent to buy or improve money-making assets (such as plants, machinery) divided by cash flow (see reference).

**Capitalization.** A general expression of a company's debt, shares outstanding, and shareholders.

**Cash Flow.** Net income minus preferred dividends and depreciation, cash flow figures provide an indication of how much money the company is keeping after expenses.

**Consensus Earnings Forecast.** A term used by Standard & Poor's and other firms denoting the average of available estimates from two thousand Wall Street analysts.

**Consolidated Balance Sheet.** A financial statement that shows the condition of a company (assets and liabilities).

**Current Assets.** The total amount of cash, liquid securities, inventories, and receivables that can be converted into cash within one year. This number provides a look at how much money and liquidity the company has for short-term emergencies or expansion. The opposite figure would be "noncurrent assets," which are largely illiquid.

**Current Liabilities.** Debt and liabilities due within one year.

**Current Price.** The previous day's closing price of a company's stock as reported by its listing exchanges.

**Current Ratio.** Current assets divided by liabilities; current ratio is one measure of a company's financial health.

**Current Yield.** A percentage return based on the annual dividend rate divided by the stock price of the previous day.

**Day Order.** An order placed with a stockbroker to buy or sell only on the day it was placed. The order expires at the end of the business day. The opposite is "good until canceled," which will stay in force until the transaction is made or the customer cancels it.

**Debt-to-Equity Ratio.** Long-term debt divided by shareholder's equity from the previous year; an important number that shows how much debt the company is carrying.

**Dividend Yield.** An annualized percentage of the company's dividend.

**Dollar-Cost Averaging.** An investment technique that requires periodic investments at regular intervals. The technique "averages out" stock prices to avoid highs or lows.

**Earnings per Share (EPS).** The company's net income or profit (before extraordinary items) divided by the average number of common shares during a given period. This number reflects the company's profitability as expressed on a per-share basis.

**Ex-Dividend.** The event triggered by a mutual fund paying distributions in the form of dividends and/or capital gains. The net asset value of the fund drops by the amount of the dividend. The ex-dividend "date" is when a stock trades without the dividend.

**FASB/Financial Accounting Standards Board.** A body that determines accounting standards for publicly held corporations.

**Growth Stock/Investing.** A stock whose earnings outpace the U.S. gross domestic product.

**Indicated Annual Dividend Rate.** A projection of the company's dividend based on recent cash payments.

**Insider Activity, Sentiment.** Stock activity conducted by the directors, officers, and key employees of a company. Activity may indicate some sentiment on the part of insiders on the health or prospects of the company.

**Institutional Holdings.** The percentage of total outstanding shares held by institutional (large) investors. Stocks held largely by institutions may be more volatile than those largely held by individuals. Institutions consist of pension funds, foundations, universities, banks, insurance companies, and large money managers.

**Loads.** Commissions on an investment product such as a mutual fund or life insurance policy. Expressed as a percentage of funds invested, they are "front end" (when you buy) or "back end" or "surrender" (when you sell). Occasionally companies charge "reinvestment" loads when you reinvest dividends or distributions; these are highly undesirable.

**Margin Account.** A brokerage account arrangement where the customer has the ability to borrow money to pay for securities, which are used as collateral. If the borrowed amount exceeds the customer's margin limits, the broker will make a "margin call"; this means that the customer must provide either more cash or more securities.

**Market Capitalization (refers to large-, mid-, and small-cap stocks).** Total shares outstanding multiplied by the previous week's closing price. This number provides an idea of how much all of the company's stock is worth.

**Market Order.** An order placed with a stockbroker to buy a security at the current price on the listing stock exchange (during business hours).

**National Association of Securities Dealers Automated Quotations (NASDAQ).** An electronic system that allows brokers to quote and trade stocks through a computer system. The system represents the second-largest stock exchange in the world. Also called the over-the-counter exchange.

**Net Income.** Income from all sources after subtracting expenses, taxes, and interest—but before deducting dividends or extraordinary items (as noted in the annual or quarterly reports).

**Penny Stocks.** These issues, which sell at under $3 per share, often carry hidden risks due to undercapitalized companies and unscrupulous brokers.

**Pink Sheets.** Listings of the smallest over-the-counter securities.

**Price-Earnings Ratio (P/E).** Common stock price divided by actual or estimated earnings per period. A relative measure of a company's price relative to earnings, the P/E should be compared to companies within its industry sector and to the S&P 500 to gauge whether it is expensive when compared to similar companies. For example, if a stock is selling for $30 and pays a $2 dividend, its P/E is fifteen to one, or fifteen times earnings.

**Quotations (Price).** Expressed as "bid" and "ask" quotes—the bid is the price offered for a stock; the ask is the price requested.

**Relative Strength.** The stock's price relative to the S&P 500. If greater than 100, the stock is performing stronger relative to the index; below 100, the opposite is the case.

**Return on Assets.** Net income divided by total assets for a given year. This is a relative measure of management performance.

**Return on Equity.** Expressed as a percentage, ROE equals the net income divided by stockholder's equity for the year indicated.

**Revenue.** Income net of excise taxes, also called sales. "Operating" revenues come from the company's main line of business excluding outside investments.

**Round Lot.** A unit of trading, typically one hundred shares. The opposite is an "odd lot." Brokers may charge additional fees for trading odd lots.

**Sales per Employee.** Revenues from the last year divided by the number of employees; a relative measure of productivity.

**Securities Investor Protection Corporation (SIPC).** An organization that insures assets held in brokerage accounts.

**Shareholder's Equity.** This shows how much of the company shareholders own minus losses.

**Shares Outstanding.** The number of shares in public hands and not held by the company's treasury.

**Split.** The action taken by a company's board of directors to divide outstanding shares into a greater number of shares. The opposite is a "reverse" split. For example, a company splitting its stock "two for one" will turn one hundred shares at $50 a share into two hundred shares at $25 a share, so the equity holding at the time of the split is the same. These actions are designed largely to encourage ownership at a lower price.

**Stop-Loss Order.** An order placed with a stockbroker to automatically sell a stock when it declines to a prestated price. This tactic is designed to prevent losses in excess of the stated "stop-loss" price.

**Street Name.** A term for securities held in the broker's name and not the customer's.

**Twelve-month (Fifty-two week) High and Low.** The highest and lowest closing prices over an annual period.

**Twelve-Month Price Relative to S&P 500.** An indication of whether the stock outperformed the S&P 500 large stock index. If greater than 1, the stock beat the S&P 500 (1 = the S&P 500's performance).

**Warrant.** A certificate giving an investor a right to purchase a set number of shares within a given period of time.

**Working Control.** A situation where a group of stockholders own at least 50 percent of a company's outstanding shares.

# RESOURCES

## PUBLICATIONS

### BOOKS

*Beating the Street* and *One Up on Wall Street*, both by Peter Lynch (Simon & Schuster). Down-to-earth investment advice for any type of investor by one of the greatest money managers of modern times.

*The Best Stocks to Own in the World*, by Gene Walden (Dearborn Financial, 1993). The author uses a selection method similar to the NAIC, choosing classic growth companies that have solid sales, earnings, franchises, and management. The book is an expanded version of his best-selling *100 Best Stocks to Own in the U.S.*

*Buying Stocks without a Broker* and *Free Lunch on Wall Street*, by Charles Carlson (McGraw-Hill). Both books focus on dividend reinvestment plans and direct-purchase stocks. Essential reading for any stock investor.

*Dividends Don't Lie*, by Geraldine Weiss (Dearborn Financial). This bible on buying dividend-rich stocks is a fine entry-level book for conservative investors looking for value.

*Improving Your Credit and Reducing Your Debt*, by Gail Liberman and Alan Lavine (John Wiley). The most useful treatment of credit and debt available.

*Individual Investor's Guide to Low-Load Mutual Funds* (International Publishing). This ample volume is a comprehensive guide to the world of low-load funds.

*Inside U.S. Business: A Concise Encyclopedia of Leading Industries*, by Philip Mattera (Irwin Professional Publishing). This reference gives you an overview of major industries and the leading players.

*How to Read a Financial Report*, by John Tracy (John Wiley & Sons). An excellent introduction to deciphering financial statements.

*Investing for Good*, by Peter Kinder, Steven Lydenberg, and Amy Domini (HarperBusiness, 1994). The quintessential guide to socially responsible investing.

*Market Movers*, by Nancy Dunnan and Jay Pack (Warner, 1993). Packed full of all sorts of signals that trigger market movements. Good background for any stock investor.

*The Way to Save*, by Ginita Wall (Owl/Henry Holt, 1993). Basic advice on how to set up your investment kitty.

*Kiplinger's 12 Steps to a Worry-Free Retirement*, by Daniel Kehrer (Kiplinger Books). The most concise and straightforward retirement planning book on the market.

*Moody's Handbook of Dividend Achievers* (Moody's Investor's Services). A must-read that not only profiles dividend growth of 325 companies, but gives insights into the companies' balance sheets.

*S&P's Directory of DRPs* (Standard & Poor's). A basic directory of DRPs.

*Security Analysis* by Graham & Dodd (McGraw-Hill). The classic text on stock selection based on value criteria. Although a ponderous and dense work, it's the mother lode of stock analysis.

*Small Stocks, Big Profits*, by Gerald Perritt (Dearborn Financial). The definitive book on investing in small-cap stocks, written by one of the leading minds in money management.

*Social Insecurity: The Crisis in America's Social Security System and How to Plan Now for Your Own Financial Survival*, by Dorcas Hardy and C. Colburn Hardy (Villard Books). If you had any delusions that Social Security will be around to finance a comfortable retirement, read this eye-opener. Written by the former commissioner of Social Security.

*Your Money or Your Life: Transforming Your Relationship with Money and Achieving Financial Independence*, by Joe Dominguez and Vicki Robin (Penguin). This seminal examination of our money/life relationships will help you square basic financial needs with life goals and aspirations.

## MAGAZINES

The following magazines are available in your public library (except for *Better Investing*) and are excellent sources of investment information.

*Better Investing* (810-583-NAIC). The official magazine of the NAIC focuses on stock picks, offering dozens of recommendations per issue, regular columnists, and guests. There are even sections for beginning investors, a "fix-it" column for clubs that want their portfolios evaluated (authored by Ralph Seger), profiles of clubs, the annual "Top 100" list of the most popular NAIC stocks, and ample resources on books, software, and other NAIC benefits. Even if you're not a member of a club, the magazine is invaluable. See listing on NAIC services in this section for subscription information.

*Consumers Digest:* 5705 N. Lincoln Ave., Chicago, IL 60659

(312-275-3590). Although largely a product-oriented buying guide, this magazine has regular features for beginning investors. An annual mutual fund buying guide sets up funds with good long-term records in portfolios. Edited by the author, it's a good resource if you're starting out and need some basic advice.

*Business Week* (800-635-1200). The best edited business magazine, this weekly features great reporting on companies, annual mutual fund rankings, the "1000 Most Valuable Companies" (by market capitalization), and sections on stock picks ("Inside Wall Street," authored by Gene Marcial), business cycles, social/corporate trends, and personal finance. Their "*Business Week* 1000" section, published in late March/early April, is a compendium for investors that includes company ratings on sales, profits, market value, assets, and undervaluation. As a companion to *Better Investing*, *Forbes*, and *Fortune*, *Business Week* should be consulted on a regular basis.

*Forbes* (800-888-9896). *Forbes* likes to buck trends with a "point of view" editorial style that leaves little doubt as to where the editors stand on the state of a company or industry. Known for their ratings of mutual funds, "Forbes 400," "Forbes Index," and industry leaders, the magazine is a font of ideas on small and mid-size companies. Look for their annual company ratings (published in late April), which ranks corporations by sales, profits, assets, market value, employment, and productivity.

*Fortune*: Time & Life Building, New York, NY 10020-1393 (800-541-1000; 212-522-1212). Having established the *Fortune* 500 in business parlance years ago, *Fortune* focuses strongly on corporate/industry trends. Like several Time Warner publications, *Fortune* concentrates on "big picture" stories. Although their stock-picking sections aren't as good as their competition, they provide a decent overview of companies and industries.

*Kiplinger's Personal Finance:* 1729 H St., NW, Washington, D.C. 20006 (800-544-0155; 202-887-6400). Formerly *Changing Times, Kiplinger's* is the blue-collar personal finance magazine, complete and unflinching. Although their investment coverage features generous profiles of mutual funds (and regular rankings), they also excel in "back of the book" features on credit, financial planning, taxes, and portfolio management.

*Money:* Time & Life Building, New York, NY 10020-1393 (800-633-9970). The Horatio Alger of personal finance magazines, *Money* presents its advice in the context of upper-middle-class readers who have plenty of disposable income and have done well with it. Consistently rates mutual funds, CDs, and credit cards.

*Smart Money:* 1790 Broadway, New York, NY 10019 (800-444-4204). Published by Dow Jones and Hearst, this newest entrant in the personal finance arena is the savviest of the group, since it's written largely by Dow Jones/*Wall Street Journal* reporters and editors. It's loaded with stock picks and cautionary advice on mutual funds and other personal finance items.

*Worth:* 575 Lexington Ave., New York, NY 10022 (800-777-1851; 800-278-5511). Published by Fidelity Investments, this is the *Vanity Fair* of personal finance magazines. Although *Worth* tends to edit more for upper-crust style than substance, it's still a good place to find Peter Lynch's advice and a host of other stock picks.

*Your Money:* 5705 N. Lincoln Ave., Chicago, IL 60659 (312-275-3590). The sister publication of *Consumers Digest,* this magazine is crisply edited and packed full of investment ideas ranging from mutual funds to collectibles. It's an omnibus of investment advice.

# NEWSLETTERS

*Best 100 Stocks Update:* P.O. Box 39373, Minneapolis, MN 55439-9781 (800-736-2970). Based on Walden's book *The 100 Best Stocks to Own in America*, this newsletter updates the status of those stocks plus international companies and mutual funds.

*The Cheap Investor:* 2549 W. Golf Rd., Suite 350, Hoffman Estates, IL 60194 (708-830-5666). A great source of information on low-priced stocks.

*DRIP Investor:* 7412 Calumet Ave., Hammond, IN 46324-2692 (219-931-6480). A lively and informative chronicler of dividend reinvestment plans. Included are model portfolios, news, direct-purchase stocks, and question and answer columns.

*Dick Davis Digest:* P.O. Box 9547, Fort Lauderdale, FL 33310 (800-654-1514). Tapping ideas from more than 450 other newsletters and reports, the digest is a topical source of investment ideas.

*Growth Stock Outlook:* P.O. Box 15381, Chevy Chase, MD 20825 (301-654-5205). Edited by the stalwart Charles Allmon, GSO features conservative stock picks that represent good values.

*Market Letter,* Wayne Hummer & Co.: 300 S. Wacker Dr., Chicago, IL (800-621-4477; 312-431-1700). Follows market trends and stocks.

*Market Logic:* 3471 North Federal, Ft. Lauderdale, FL 33306 (800-442-9000). Published by the Institute for Econometric Research, ML is adept at tracking market trends. Their companion newsletter, *Investor's Digest,* summarizes recommendations from a variety of newsletters.

*The Moneypaper, the Monthly Guide for the Self-Reliant Investor:* 1010 Mamaroneck Ave., Mamaroneck, NY 10543 (914-381-5400). A diverse and interesting newsletter that covers everything from DRP and direct-purchase stocks to market overviews and company profiles. Their ample *Guide to Dividend Reinvestment Plans*, which lists 871 companies, is available to subscribers for $9.

*Morningstar Investor:* 225 W. Wacker Dr., Chicago, IL 60606 (800-876-5005; 312-696-6000). This newsletter focuses on the best five hundred mutual funds (closed- and open-end) as rated by Morningstar's risk/return "star" system. News and sample portfolios are also covered. Perhaps the best mutual fund newsletter in the business.

*Plain Talk Investor:* 1500 Skokie Blvd., Suite 203, Northbrook, IL 60062 (800-530-1500). Filled with market commentary and cycle analysis, this personality-plus newsletter features "Personal Best" and "High Risk/High Reward" portfolios.

*Stock Trader's Almanac:* Six Deer Trail, Old Tappan, NJ 07675 (800-477-3400). Edited for more than twenty-seven years by newsletter stalwart Yale Hirsch, the publication tracks cycles, averages, and market indicators.

## NEWSPAPERS (DAILIES IN BOLDFACE)

*Barron's* (800-544-0422). A weekly tabloid, this witty and insightful newspaper is the most entertaining source of investment information on Wall Street. Regular features cover individual stocks, industries, and managers. In the first quarter, the "Roundtable" sports some of the best investors in the world offering their investment picks for the coming year. Peerless in its "tabular" coverage of every financial and commodity market, *Barron's* is required reading for every investor. Having published several articles in this weekly over the years, I can tell you the editing is lively and first rate.

*Individual Investor* (212-689-2777). Inexpensive and packed with stock ideas, the monthly covers everything from small stocks to bargain-priced blue chips.

**Investor's Business Daily** (800-831-2525). While *The Wall Street Journal* has evolved into an international business newspaper, *Investor's Business Daily* has grown into a scrappy competitor that takes a hard look at markets and the economy. A good second or third read for current information.

**The Wall Street Journal** (800-221-1940). Still the leading daily business periodical, the *Journal* has enhanced its coverage of big trends, companies, and the intricate dealings of Wall Street. Like *Barron's*, it provides complete coverage of every market. Its back section features on marketing and personal investing have improved dramatically in recent years and are worth scouting for investment ideas.

## FINANCIAL ADVICE AND REFERRALS

Bankcard Holders of America (703-389-5445). This nonprofit group provides lists of low-rate and no-fee credit cards.

Bureau of the Public Debt/Treasury Securities Information (202-874-4000). For information on buying U.S. Treasury securities directly—and thus avoiding a broker's commission—this line will provide rates and information.

Broker/Planner Background Checks. The best route is to call your state securities department. You can call the NASAA for the number at (202)737-0900. A less dependable source is the NASD's CRD service at (800)289-9999.

EE U.S. Savings Bonds (800-US-BONDS). Provides rate and purchase information.

Institute of Certified Financial Planners (800-282-7526). This trade group will refer you to a certified financial planner in your area.

American Institute of Certified Public Accountants (AICPA), Personal Financial Planning Division, Harborside Financial Center: 201 Plaza III, Jersey City, NJ 07311-3881 (201-938-3000). The AICPA will provide a list of certified public accountants in your area who have at least 250 hours of experience per year prior to passing a six-hour exam.

International Association for Financial Planning: Two Concourse Parkway, Suite 800, Atlanta, GA 30328 (800-945-4237; 404-395-1605). This trade group will provide listings of its top planners, all of whom have passed rigorous tests and reviews.

International Board of Standards and Practices for Certified Financial Planners (303-830-7543). This group can tell you if a planner claiming to have earned the "certified financial planner" (CFP) title has been approved to use it. They also register complaints against CFPs.

Institute of Certified Financial Planners (800-282-7526). The group will provide a referral list of certified financial planners in your area and a helpful brochure.

National Association of Personal Financial Advisers: 1130 Lake Cook Road, Suite 105, Buffalo Grove, IL 60089 (708-537-7722; 800-366-2732).

This group represents fee-only financial planners, meaning they don't receive a commission on what they sell. They will provide a list of planners in your area, a questionnaire to select planners, and a brochure about NAPFA.

Ibbotson Associates: 225 N. Michigan Ave., Suite 700, Chicago, IL 60601-7676 (312-616-1620). They're the research people who track the long-term performance of T-bills, stocks, bonds, and inflation, among many other things. A truly dependable source for investment data on broad investment categories.

Moody's Investors Service: 99 Church St., New York, NY 10007 (800-342-5647). With Standard & Poor's and Value Line, Moody's completes the troika of mainstream investment reference houses. Moody's rates bonds and stocks through a number of different publications, most of which are available in the library. Of special note is their handbook, which uses a price score system in evaluating nine hundred stocks.

Morningstar ADR, Japanese Stocks, Variable Annuity Reports (800-876-5005). The financial rating company rates and reviews these investments in detail. (Also see "Mutual Fund Rating Services.")

William O'Neil & Co.: P.O. Box 66919, Los Angeles, CA 90066 (310-448-6843). O'Neil's Daily Graphs service lists more than 1,600 stocks. The company also publishes *Investor's Business Daily* and conducts investment workshops throughout the country.

SEC-Registered Investment Advisors (202-272-3100). The agency will tell you if the planner is registered as a "registered investment advisor." If so, the planner must show you his/her "Form ADV," which discloses all business and investment interests.

S&P Reports OnDemand (800-292-0808; 800-221-5277). A definitive resource that rates and reports on more than 4,400 companies and 80 industries and provides more than 10,000 price and index charts. This order-by-phone service allows you to order as little as one company or industry report. Other key resources include the Standard Reports, *Stock Market Encyclopedia*, Watching Service, and *Stock Guide*. S&P is perhaps one of the most versatile research houses on Wall Street, producing everything from benchmark indexes (the S&P 500, Mid-Cap Index, and so on) to specific recommendations.

Social Security Administration (800-772-1213). The agency will send you information on obtaining your "Personal Earnings and Benefit Estimate Statement," which shows how much you've contributed to the system and the paltry benefit you're likely to receive (assuming the system stays solvent and benefits aren't cut).

*Value Line Investment Survey*: 711 Third Ave., New York, NY 10017 (800-833-0046). Long the staple of stock investors, Value Line is still a classic one-stop resource. Combining their famous graphs (showing stock splits) and write-ups, the service also features a section of three hundred NYSE-listed stocks selling at under $20 a share. The hallmark of the service, however, is still its analyses, "appreciation potential" and "timeliness" ratings, which are of the most value to individual investors. Since it's rare not to find *Value Line* surveys in most libraries, you probably won't have to worry about its $525/year subscription price.

## Mutual Fund Rating Services

Morningstar: 225 W. Wacker Dr., Chicago, IL 60606 (800-876-5005; 312-696-6000). The leading fund rating service, Morningstar has expanded to cover nearly every aspect of fund investing. Not only does the service provide performance analyses, it also breaks out tax liabilities, management changes, risk/return numbers, and holdings by industry sector.

The main product, *Morningstar Mutual Funds*, is a constantly updated biweekly newsletter that is kept in a binder. Although a bit overwhelming for most individual investors, it offers a comprehensive look at the industry, evaluating one to three fund groups every issue. A much more boiled down version of the flagship is available in the service's *Investor* newsletter.

The hallmark of Morningstar's system is its "star" rating system, which balances risk and return. A "five" in the system would signal a fund with the best possible performance and the lowest relative risk. Every statistical measure of risk, return, and indexes is included on every Morningstar page.

For computer users, Morningstar data is available in a CD-ROM (OnDisc) and floppy disk (OnFloppy) product. The software with the data allows you to pose "what if" questions, plot your own graphs, and come up with customized fund lists based on any number of criteria (asset size, return, risk, etc.).

Morningstar also rates closed-end funds and hosts excellent biannual conferences that feature the best fund managers in the business. Having attended every conference and used nearly all of Morningstar's resources for the past five years, I can tell you they are the best in the business and full of ideas for any level of investor.

Other Morningstar services of note include their OnDemand product, which allows you to request information on single funds over the phone and access to company ratings on 3,500 funds on American Online (800-827-6364).

Value Line Mutual Fund Survey: 220 E. 42nd St., New York, NY 10017-5891 (800-284-7607). This new service looks remarkably like Morningstar but doesn't feel like it. Although they cover some two thousand funds, their commentary is not as incisive, nor do they perform tax liability ratings on the funds. They also lack the powerful companion software products.

Like Morningstar, the Value Line product is a binder newsletter with one-page summaries of funds laid out pretty much the same way (only with slightly better graphics than Morningstar). All performance and relative measures are included on every page. One useful feature of Value Line—which Morningstar doesn't have yet—is an "investment planning worksheet" that allows you to chart risk and match funds that meet your risk profile. They also throw in a monthly newsletter and a book, *How to Invest in Mutual Funds*. Other key sections include "Market Outlook," "Fund Close-ups," "Fund Selectors," "News Briefs," and "Performance Reviews."

NOTE: Every major business and financial newspaper/magazine runs regular coverage on mutual funds. Included are *Barron's*, *Business Week*, *Financial World*, *Forbes*, *Fortune*, *Kiplinger's Personal Finance*, *Consumers Digest*, *Consumers Reports*, *Money*, *Smart Money*, *The Wall Street Journal*, *Worth*, and *Your Money*. The most complete analysis, however, is found in *Barron's*, *Business Week*, *Forbes*, *Money*, and *Smart Money*. Mutual fund net asset values are found in the financial sections of daily newspapers. For even more in-depth analysis consult Morningstar Mutual Funds or their *Five-Star Investor* newsletter or Value Line's Mutual Fund service. Other important directories include

*No-Load Investors Mutual Fund Guide*
*Mutual Fund Encyclopedia* (Perritt)
*Investment Company Institute Guide to Mutual Funds*
*Mutual Fund Education Alliance*

## Mutual Fund Networks

These fund networks allow you to consolidate all your records and "trade" among funds through a phone call. Their greatest advantage is selection and convenience. All rates and conditions are subject to change.

### Fidelity FundsNetwork (800-544-9697)

The largest mutual fund group offers funds outside of its own group, which covers more than three hundred funds from thirty-two other "families." The network offers non-transaction fee (NTF) funds to customers who want access to the funds but don't want to pay additional charges. These networks cut costs to investors by receiving rebates from the fund companies from 0.25 percent to 0.35 percent of assets held in their accounts. In other words, the network is a one-stop-shopping distribution channel for smaller fund groups. The Fidelity group, which is about half the size of the Schwab program, offers funds from Blanchard, Bull & Bear, Dreman, Dreyfus, Founders, Oberweis, PBHG Growth, and Wasatch. Some of the Fidelity funds may overlap with the Schwab network. Both are constantly adding to their networks. The main benefit of the Fidelity network is the ability to buy several popular Fidelity low-load funds without sales charges for retirement accounts. Exceptions are made for the Magellan, New Millennium, and Select portfolios.

Like the other programs, Fidelity restricts trading of the funds within the network. You are limited to four short-term trades on non-Fidelity funds and four round-trip trades on Fidelity funds. You will be charged a transaction fee for the fifth trade (or more) on non-Fidelity funds, and the company reserves the right to refuse your fifth trade request on the Fidelity funds (per account in a rolling twelve-month period).

### Charles Schwab Mutual Fund OneSource (800-266-5623)

This is the premier mutual funds network service, offering more than eight hundred funds. Although you can't get into every fund through this service, it's a good way to avoid a heap of sales charges. Like the other services, you have a choice of non-transaction fee (NTF) or transaction fee funds. More than two hundred of the total funds are NTF. Major fund groups offered include Benham, Berger, Evergreen, Federated, IAI, Invesco, Janus, Lexington, Neuberger & Berman, Oakmark, Steinroe, Strong, Twentieth Century, United Services, and Warburg. Note the absence of the Fidelity group, which has its own network.

Schwab's restrictions are similar to Fidelity's, limiting your participation to four short-term trades (buy and sell or "round trip") within a twelve-month calendar period. There are no trading restrictions if you hold a fund at least twelve months before another transaction. For exceeding the restrictions, you'll have to pay transaction fees, which range from 0.6 percent of principal to a minimum $29 commission. All rules and fund offerings are subject to change.

### Jack White & Co. (800-323-3263)

This deep-discount broker has an impressive funds network and is worth considering to find some of the smaller funds. More than 700 funds from 50 different families are available, 317 on an NTF basis. White is also the most lenient on trading: they impose a transaction fee only after a sixty-day holding period, but no additional fees after that. The transaction charges range from $27 to $50, depending upon the asset size of the trade (from $10,000 to $25,000 plus). Fund groups include Alliance, Babson, Federated, Loomis Sayles, Merriman, Selected, and Value Line.

## Investment Groups

**American Association of Individual Investors: 625 N. Michigan Ave., Chicago, IL 60611-3110 (312-280-0170).** Annual membership $49; lifetime membership $490. Unlike the NAIC, which provides the method for stock picking, AAII provides an interesting forum for investors of every stripe. Although emphasis is on common stock ownership, the group offers analyses on everything from CDs to variable annuities.

Like the NAIC, AAII's support publications are numerous and stimulating. Not only does the group publish a number of useful publications, it sponsors seminars across the country to educate its membership.

An independent, not-for-profit organization founded in 1978, the AAII has more than 160,000 members. One of the best benefits of membership is its *AAII Journal* (ten times/year), which features analyses and commentary by experts such as Peter Lynch, Mark Hulbert, and other leading financial professionals. The journal is comprehensive in that it covers every aspect of investing in a financial planning perspective. While it tends to be a bit academic in tone, it's a useful resource for any investors.

Having known one of AAII's co-founders and interviewed their principals over the last ten years, I've found their programs to be well prepared and rewarding. Unlike the NAIC, which is highly decentralized and mostly a volunteer operation, the AAII produces most of its programs and research from its Chicago headquarters. Their executives are also well compensated and extremely visible in the national financial media. This is a group, however, that is more interested in providing the tools and ideas for successful investing on an individual basis than the club-oriented NAIC.

Following is a list of AAII membership benefits:

- *Local Chapter Membership.* **More than fifty chapters are spread out throughout the country and meet periodically. Subgroups focus on computer investing.**
- **Individual Investor's Guide to Low-Load Mutual Funds. An annual guide to eight hundred mutual funds with ratings and comments.**
- **Year-End Tax Strategy Guide. The booklet covers tax planning for investors.**
- *AAII Quoteline.* **Members can obtain real-time stock quotes via telephone.**
- *Dividend Reinvestment Programs.* **A free listing of companies offering DRPs is provided.**
- **AAII Journal. As previously mentioned, the magazine focuses on improving overall investment results.**
- *Shadow Stock Coverage.* **A feature of the *AAII Journal*, this is a list of specially selected stocks that are chosen because they are not covered by most analysts yet have good prospects.**
- *Computer Bulletin Boards.* **For members who use computers, this service offers free programs and chances to talk to other members.**
- *Stock Brokerage Survey.* **Each January the leading brokers are surveyed on commissions.**

- *Credit Card.* A no-fee gold MasterCard features rental car insurance and product warranty protection.

AAII services available at additional cost:

- *Computerized Investing.* For an additional $30 membership fee, you receive a bimonthly newsletter that reviews stock-picking software packages.
- *Stock Investor.* Quarterly updates on more than seven thousand stocks available on computer diskette. Offered at a discount.
- *Investment Seminars.* Available to members at a discount, these educational programs cover different phases of investing and are offered through the fifty chapters. The seminars also include generous materials and are available on video.
- *Publications Discounts.* Magazines and software are discounted for members. S&P reports available at no cost "for a number of corporations."
- *Home Study.* Starts from the basics and moves into advanced levels of investment theory for members. Available at "reduced cost."
- *Quarterly Mutual Fund Update.* The optional service updates funds listed in the *AAII's Low-Load Guide.*
- *Bank Money Market Account.* The FDIC-insured fund is guaranteed to produce a "yield above the average of all money market mutual funds. . . ."

Investors Alliance: 219 Commercial Blvd., P.O. Box 11209, Ft. Lauderdale, FL 33339-1209 (305-491-5100). One-year membership $49; computer membership $89; lifetime membership $520. Similar to the AAII, this nonprofit education group serves forty-eight thousand and offers a number of services. Although unreviewed by the author, it appears to be a good value. Members receive:

- subscription to *Investor's Journal* magazine
- mutual fund and stock research ("personalized")
- investor hot lines
- computer screens for undervalued stocks and funds
- directory of one thousand DRP plans
- self-study tutorial
- discount broker directory
- discounts on investment publications
- mutual fund databank on two thousand funds
- stock analysis software
- charting software
- portfolio management software
- computerized DRP directory

**National Association of Investors Corporation: P.O. Box 220, Royal Oak, MI 48071 (810-583-6242).** Annual individual membership $35; club membership $35 plus $11 per member; lifetime membership $550; computer group $30; magazine subscription $20/12 issues.

For more than forty-four years the NAIC has been the Jeffersonian ideal of the investment club movement. Lightly staffed yet unusually supportive (with almost no bureaucracy), the NAIC offers a variety of services and publications to meet the needs of nearly any type of investor.

Clearly, the more than ten thousand clubs and regional councils constitute the driving force behind the NAIC. But much of the inspiration for local organization comes from NAIC headquarters in the Detroit area, which is the source of most of the national programs and resources.

Education is, without doubt, the most powerful aspect of the NAIC's focus. Directors and executives of the NAIC from coast to coast consistently stress the mantra "We're here to learn to make money." All of the NAIC's materials reflect that premise.

The NAIC also recommends stocks through its Securities Review Committee, magazine, and Investment Advisory Service, all of which operate independently. For a group that flouts Wall Street's outsized advice industry, the NAIC has done quite well; its recommendations (through the review committee) have beaten the Dow Jones Industrial Average twenty-five times over the last thirty-six years.

As an educational organization, NAIC is first rate. Their investor fairs, information reports, and support materials are written for all levels of investor. For active investors, the Low-Cost Investment Plan and magazine are worth the membership fee alone.

Here is an overview of NAIC offerings:

- *Stock Study Tools*/Stock Selection Guide & Report. This is the main tool that members use to analyze a stock and determine if it's worth buying. It employs the NAIC's "Rule of Five" (five companies analyzed for five-year future) and several fundamental methods. The four-page form walks investors through goals, evaluating management, price, and trend analyses. It's the single most useful tool the group offers aside from the manual.
- Investors Manual. This is the NAIC bible, which explains the fundamentals of NAIC stock picking. There are two edi-

tions—club and individual. A *First-Time Investor Manual* is also available.

- Accounting Manual. A bookkeeping primer, this essential reference tells how to set up and track portfolios.
- *Investment Advisory Service*. If you can't get enough ideas from *Better Investing* or any of the aforementioned resources, this premium (additional cost) service can help. The quarterly service (priced at $99 per year, or $35 for a three-month trial) picks and follows a select group of eighty stocks. What's convenient about the service is that the issues are preselected using NAIC methods, so you're dealing with a pool of stocks in which you don't have to do the legwork and initial research (a blessing or a curse, depending upon how active an investor you are). The service, run by longtime NAIC director Ralph Seger, uses seven rankings: yield, P/E ratio, relative value, upside/downside ratio, pay-back time, P/E percent of growth, and total return. Generally, this is a great companion resource that's most useful in determining good times to buy a particular issue and determining under-valued stocks. Over the years, the service has done well, often beating the S&P 500, so it's worth the investment as a monitoring tool and idea bank.
- Better Investing. As described in the magazine section, the monthly features news, stock picks, and club activities. It's also fun to read, gearing its style to novice and intermediate investors.
- Better Investing BITS. Focusing on the use of computers in investing, the ten-times-per-year magazine features software reviews and tips. Information on spreadsheets, seminars, and stock screens is also covered.
- *Computer Service, Group, and Software*. The organization

sponsors computer users groups, sells its own accounting and portfolio management software, and offers other packages. Although there's an additional fee to join the computer group, the membership provides software discounts, a newsletter (BITS), and special educational meetings and fairs. There's even an "Online Investor Forum" for those with modems and a free introductory package on CompuServe. Their "One Stop" publication lists all of the available software and free shareware. Of special interest are the software versions of the *Stock Selection Guide, Stock Comparison Guide, Portfolio Management Guide*, portfolio evaluation, and review technique. All of these programs are contained in their "Investor's Toolkit." Prices range from $29 to $49 per program. If you just want stock analysis and graphing, consider their "SSG Combined" package, which is a higher-end product ranging from $149 for computer group members to $189 for nonmembers. If you want, you can just buy demonstration disks of the packages as a trial. The following is a list of what's available:

Investor's Toolkit—SSG Master Module
Investor's Toolkit—Stock Comparison Guide
Investor's Toolkit—Portfolio Management
Investor's Toolkit—PERT
Investor's Toolkit—Complete
SSG PLUS
PERT for DOS
SSG Combined
SSG Combined Demo
Take Stock
NAIC Club Accounting

NAIC Club Accounting Demo
NAIC Datafiles—quarterly
NAIC Datafiles—yearly
PERT Datafiles
Free Software Brochures

Software is available on 5¼-inch and 3½-inch formats in
IBM, IBM-Windows, Macintosh, and Apple II.

- *Investor Information Reports.* These one-page reports give
  you a comprehensive yet concise breakdown of a company's
  price ranges, balance sheet, financial highlights, company
  contacts, visual analysis of earnings per share/revenues,
  price/earnings history, yield, and management review (pre-
  tax profit on sales). They are worth the price of membership
  alone.
- *Regional Councils.* These are the volunteer subgroups within the NAIC that put on most of the educational programs
  and investor fairs on a local basis. They also provide help in
  getting clubs started.
- *Free Brochures.* If you feel you're not ready to commit to a
  membership, request some of these NAIC brochures:

1. *An Educational and Investment Opportunity for You*
2. *Suggested Steps for Starting an Investment Club*
3. *Investor Advisory Service*
4. *Low-Cost Investment Plan*
5. *Stock Study Tools*
6. *NAIC Computer Group*
7. *One-Stop* (software listings)

**National Center for Financial Education: P.O. Box 34070, San Diego, CA 92163-4070 (619-232-8811).** A nonprofit group dedicated to financial planning, the NCFE provides some of the best basic information on money management and credit. Their *Credit Repair and Improvement Guide* is a worthwhile read if you need to get on solid footing with your credit cards. Ask for their *Money Book Store Catalog.*

**National Consumers League: 815 15th St., NW, #928-N, Washington, D.C. 20005.** A co-sponsor of the National Fraud Information Center, the NCL publishes a few free publications on investing. Ask for their *Putting the Pieces Together: Solving the Financial Puzzle,* which is an excellent primer on financial reports.

# INDEX

and dividends in driving long-
term stocks, 165, 167
market cycles and, 186–90
timing and, 213, 215–16
and what good stocks look like,
132–33, 136
Internal Revenue Service (IRS),
19, 48
International Harvester
Corporation, 15
international investing:
and balancing risk and reward,
143
diversification and, 145, 152–55
McDonald's and, 127
market timing and, 183
and what good stocks look like,
88, 90, 94, 98, 115, 117, 127,
129–30
Intrinsic Value club, management
rated by, 121–25
Invesco Strategic Health Sciences
Portfolio, 248
Investment Advisors Act, 51
investment clubs:
advice on, 48, 77–80
of all women, 13
appeal of, xv
auditing accounts of, 76
average annual returns of, 2
and being responsible investor,
81
common questions about,
71–74
contributing to, 80
diversity of membership of, 75
duration of meetings of, 72
as educational venture, 8–10,
39, 74, 138
finding one to join, 71
habits of highly effective, 74
how they do better, 25–31

irreconcilable differences in,
75–76
learning patience and
perseverance in, 11
majority rules in, 76
in making good decisions,
73–74
mother of all, 35–48
number of officers of, 73
organization of, 38–40
points of discussion at meetings
of, 70
prevalence of, 2–3
profiles of members of, 3–4
rereading and updating bylaws
of, 77
sizes of, 79–80
smooth running of, 69–81
as social venture, 39, 74
starting investments for
members of, 71
starting meetings of, 72–73
troubleshooting for, 74–77
typical meeting agendas of, 70
universal appeal of, 4
why it is good idea, 2–3
Investment Company Institute, 21
Investment Data, 237
*Investment Quality Trends*, 157,
171–72
investments, investing, and
investors:
accessibility of, 10
bottom up, 185
broadening skills in, 80
common sense in, xi
devotion to learning about, 3
getting organized for, 241–45
individuals as, 5, 28–31, 52,
245–46
long-term, 23, 26–28, 30–31,
35–36, 87

# 302 THE INVESTMENT CLUB BOOK